Chinese Baking
at Home

Chinese Baking
at Home

600 Days Sweet, Savory & Simple Recipes for
Mooncakes, Milk Bread, Mochi, and More
Inspired by Chinese Bakeries

A Cookbook

By Petry Kones

CONTENTS

INTRODUCTION

Chinese cuisine (Chinese meals) originated in various parts of Asia and has since spread to many countries around the world. Because of the vast differences in geography and culture between China's various regions, there are many different food styles to choose from. In the United States, there are eight major regional types of food to choose from. Chinese cuisine typically consists of two or more basic elements: the first is a complex carbohydrate or flour, which is referred to as a staple meal in Chinese, and the second is a variety of vegetables, meat, seafood, or other ingredients that are served alongside the carbohydrate or flour.

The majority of Chinese cuisine is heavily reliant on rice. However, wheat-based foods such as pasta and steamed bread predominate in northern China, whereas rice predominates in southern China, according to the World Food Report. Chopsticks are the primary feeding utensil in Traditional Chinese cuisine for solid foods, while a large, plain spoon is used for sauces and other liquids. Veganism is not uncommon or uncommon in China, but it is only practiced by a small percentage of the population, similar to how it is practiced in the United States and Europe.

Baked goods have been an integral part of Chinese cuisine for as long as anyone can remember. No other cooking technique can completely replace the process of baking. To bring out the flavor of foods and create delectable dishes, it is necessary to use this technique. Baking has evolved into an art form in Chinese cuisine, requiring both skill and intuition to achieve success. It takes years of hard work and dedication to achieve perfection in this field of work.

In Chinese cooking, frying and boiling are not the only methods of preparation. It is all about transforming your ingredients into a delectable piece of food, and it accomplishes this by employing a variety of techniques to make the food appear appetizing. When it comes to making their dishes visually appealing, Chinese bakers are known to be particularly inventive. They intend to use techniques such as brushing egg whites on top of a pastry or using sugar powders to create patterns that are both visually appealing and delicious.

Traditional Chinese baking differs from Western baking in that it does not use any sugar or cream, instead of relying on dried fruit (mostly dried apri-

1

cots) for sweetness; whereas Western baking relies on sugar to make the dough tender and moisten the finished product with butter or cream cheese frosting, whereas traditional Chinese baking uses dried fruit (mostly dried apricots) for sweetness

Many Chinese dishes, whether spicy or mild, have a common foundation. "The holy trinity of Chinese cuisine is ginger, garlic, and chili," as the saying goes. The wok is the heart of Chinese cooking, and it is required for any stir-fry to be successful. There is virtually no limit to the number of traditional meals that can be produced by a simple wok on the stovetop: ginger meat, sticky rice, and meat chow fun, to name a few. The quick method can help preserve the nutrients in the vegetables while also lowering the amount of fuel used.

In cooking, Chinese cuisine is one of the most well-known, having a long history and holding an important place among the Chinese cultural resources. It is well-known throughout the entire world. The introduction of Chinese cuisine has evolved over centuries, resulting in a wealth of cultural knowledge characterized by a careful selection of ingredients, precise preparation, careful attention to the level of heat, and substantial nourishment. The evolution and diversity of Chinese cuisine are also a result of the country's long historical development. With each passing generation, new techniques were developed, and eventually, the art of food preparation reached its pinnacle.

Chinese baking is unquestionably delicious, and it is a traditional food in China that is enjoyed by the majority of the population. Cakes made traditionally are available throughout China, but the styles vary depending on their origin.

PART 1

CHINESE BAKERY FUNDAMENTALS

BASICS OF CHINESE CUISINE

Since its founding four thousand years ago, the Chinese people have developed a vibrant culture, of which Chinese cuisine is an important component. The majority of foreign visitors to China are completely blown away by the cuisine of the country. Aspects of Chinese cuisine such as color, aroma, and taste are all important. Chinese chefs make an effort to coordinate the colors of their dishes to make them appear more visually appealing. Some meals are straightforward, while others are bursting with flavor. A Chinese restaurant's table is usually very bright and visually appealing.

In Chinese cuisine, the way the food tastes is extremely important. When it comes to making food smell healthy, chefs use spices and the ingredients in a recipe. The most distinguishing characteristic of Chinese cuisine, on the other hand, is its flavor. Chinese cuisine is delicious because it is prepared using various methods that provide a great deal of satisfaction to the palate. Chinese cuisine has a diverse range of ingredients, allowing Chinese chefs to be more creative in their preparation. These consist of various grains, fruits, and meat from a variety of animals, among others. Stir-frying is the most widely used cooking technique today. Chinese cuisine can be divided into eight major categories. All eight branches place a strong emphasis on the culinary excellence and artistic elegance of Chinese cuisine.

HISTORY OF CHINESE CUISINE

In China, food and its preparation have progressed to the point of being considered an artistic endeavor. Regardless of their socioeconomic status, people in China consider tasty and nutritious meals to be a basic requirement. "Food is the most basic requirement of the citizens," according to an ancient Chinese proverb.

Over centuries, this craft has been refined and refined. Although Chinese cuisine first appeared in the 15th century BC during the Shang dynasty, it was not until Yi Yin, the first Party Leader, that it gained widespread acceptance. Both of China's dominant ideologies had significant effects on the country's macroeconomic background, but it is less well established that they have impacted the development of the country's creative industries.

It was important to Confucius that cooking and eating had both cultural and intellectual aspects to them. In Chinese culture, inviting guests into your home while ensuring enough food on hand is considered common courtesy. In his writings, Confucius developed codes for cooking and dining etiquette, the majority of which have survived to the present day. For example, slicing bite-sized chunks of meat and vegetables during the food manufacturing process rather than using a knife at dinner is considered impolite.

Instead of sampling the various components, Confucius advocated combining ingredients and flavorings to create a cohesive dish from start to finish. His primary concern was the preservation of harmony. He asserted and demonstrated that there could be no flavor without the use of several different ingredients together. He also emphasized the importance of the dish's overall appearance, including color, shape, and design. Particularly noteworthy is that preparing food became an art rather than a chore, and he subscribed to the philosophy of "survive to eat" rather than "eat to survive."

Tao's nutritional aspects of food and cooking were of particular interest, who advocated for more research into this area. Taoists were much more concerned with the types of proteins that were life-giving than they were with the flavor of the proteins.

For thousands of years, the Chinese have been aware that many roots, herbs, fungi, and crops possess medicinal qualities. As a result, they have informed the world that undercooking food destroys its nutritional value, and they have discovered that foods with a pleasant taste can also have therapeutic properties.

HISTORY OF TRADITIONAL DISHES OF CHINESE FOOD

Since approximately 5000 BC, Chinese cuisine has had a long and illustrious history. Having been in existence for such a long period, the Chinese have developed their own method of food preparation. It has become more sophisticated to recognize materials to produce optimal blends, develop multi-phased preparation strategies, and administer flavoring in multiple phases. It is known that the ancient Chinese ate a well-balanced diet, and we can infer from historical evidence that agriculture in China began approximately 5,000 years ago, if not earlier.

Chinese cuisine is well-known for its adaptability and diversity of flavors. Since prehistoric times, food has been at the center of social communication, and many modern meals, with their diverse aromas and tastes, can be traced back to ancient Chinese food practices. In China, food is frequently regarded as an art form, with particular emphasis on the preparation and presentation of food.

Even though vegetables were scarce in ancient China, they played an important role in preparing various food types. Because they managed it, they ate vegetables with their staple meal of rice every day. China is regarded as one of the world's largest producers of the first wine, accounting for about a quarter of global production. Since its inception, wine has been imbued with historical and emotional significance, serving as a symbol of political and social life and artistic ideas.

Pigeon and various other meats such as beef and lamb and duck, chicken, and pigeon, among others, are the most popular in China. China's people have been consuming pork since at least 4000 or 3000 BC when the animal was indigenous. Drinking tea is considered an elegant art form in China, and there are numerous customs and traditions associated with it. An additional traditional Chinese dish is noodle soup. Noodles have been around since the Eastern Han Dynasty, and they are still popular today. In China's history, agricultural production appears to have played a significant role. For example, ancient agricultural activities are thought to have played a key role in the country's political, financial, cultural, and ideological advancements.

5

NUTRITIONAL INFORMATION AND BENEFITS OF CHINESE FOOD

Food in China is not only nutrient-dense, but it is also well-balanced, supplying all of the nutrients the body and bloodstream require to remain in good health. According to the Chinese, many vegetables and a small slice of meat can be fairly designed into a meal. Meat is important because it provides a source of refined carbohydrates to the diet. Chinese foods are low in fat, refined carbohydrates, and cholesterol, allowing our bodies to recognize when they have reached their maximum capacity. Individuals who eat Chinese food are more likely to consume an appropriate amount of food and avoid overindulging in calorie intake. Chinese cuisine, which places a strong emphasis on liquid foods, also aids in regulating food consumption.

All Chinese meals are prepared by the yin (cooling wet and moist products) and yang (heat-producing foods) theories of food production. A delicate balance of yin and yang components is used to prepare almost every dish in Chinese cuisine. Carbohydrates are yin in nature, while protein-rich foods are yang in nature. For many years, people have been drinking tea because of its potential benefits in the treatment of cardiovascular disease.

Chinese chefs haven't forgotten the ancient belief that certain ingredients, such as mushrooms, have medicinal properties, the relationship between metabolism and cancer risk.

KEY INGREDIENTS OF CHINESE FOOD

Traditional Chinese cuisine achieves its iconic status by creating the perfect balance of spicy, sour, salty, and savory flavors, so you face the risk of disrupting this fine balance by replacing core ingredients. Here is a list of key ingredients used in Chinese cuisine.

- Dried chilies
- Fermented black beans
- White rice vinegar
- Shaoxing rice wine
- Light soy sauce
- Chinese five-spice
- Chili bean sauce
- Dark soy sauce
- Sichuan peppercorns
- Sesame oil
- Dried mushrooms
- Oyster sauce

INGREDIENTS

In terms of flavor and texture, Chinese takeout recipes are a far cry from their authentic counterparts in the cuisine. Chinese chefs don't waste any ingredients, and they're not afraid to experiment with unusual ingredients such as pig ears, chicken feet, and duck blood to create delectable dishes for their customers. Takeout has been adapted to better suit the tastes of the more conservative Westerner, with the following modifications: Overall, westernized Chinese cuisine is perceived as being fattening and lacking in flavor, owing to the absence of spices in the preparation process.

Vegetables, rice, and soybeans are the primary ingredients in authentic Chinese cuisine, whereas Chinese takeout focuses on side dishes and condiments. Among the ingredients that have been Americanized in recipes are many western-style vegetables and dairy products such as carrots, broccoli, onion, tomato, and feta cheese. 'All-American' foods include canned fruits such as pineapple and sweet caramelized sauces, which are both considered to be "authentically American." When compared to the extensive selection of seafood options available in traditional Chinese cuisine, takeouts have a limited selection of seafood options. Although there are differences, Chinese takeout is undeniably popular and has come full circle, finding acceptance even in the Far East, where it first gained popularity.

Here are some of the ingredients you'll typically find in authentic Chinese recipes as well as Chinese takeout.

Soy Sauce

Fermented soy beans are used in the production of all three types of soy sauce: light soy sauce, dark soy sauce, and regular soy sauce. Light soy sauce is lighter in color, but it has a stronger saltiness than regular soy sauce. Dark soy sauce has been fermented for a longer period of time than light soy sauce. A rich caramel color and a less salty, slightly sweet flavor distinguish it from other caramels. Regular soy sauce is a medium-bodied sauce that falls somewhere between light and dark sauces.

Cooking Oil

Although deep flying is not commonly used in Chinese cooking, a variety of oils are employed. Peanut oil is used for its added fragrance, which is why it is so popular. It is also possible to use com and soy oil. Walnut oil is particularly popular among pregnant women because of its nourishing properties. As an alternative to frying, sesame oil is used to enhance the flavor of dishes. It is typically drizzled over dishes before serving.

Ginger, garlic, and scallions are among the ingredients (spring onion)

The fresh form of these is used in a variety of ways — whole, crushed, grated, or chopped. As well as being used for flavor and to remove "fishiness," they are also used for their medicinal properties.

5-Spice Powder is a spice that is used in cooking:

A flavorful blend of spices that everyone enjoys. A blend of fennel, peppercorns, star anise, cinnamon, and cloves are used to make it.

Rice Vinegar

This is the type of ingredient that is traditionally used in Chinese recipes. It is available in two colors: white and black. It gives Asian dishes a distinct flavor that is hard to replicate.

Oyster Sauce

Oysters and soy sauce are combined to create a rich, thick, brown sauce. It enhances the flavor of a variety of dishes.

Cornstarch

Sauces are commonly thickened by combining cornstarch and water. The cornstarch and water slurry is usually added to the ingredients while they are simmering in order to achieve the perfect amount of sauce to coat the ingredients evenly. This ingredient is also employed in the preparation of crispy coatings for fried meats, vegetables, and seafood.

Salt

In Chinese cuisine, salt is extremely important. It brings the flavors of all foods to life. (This is one of the reasons why some doctors forbid patients from eating Chinese food if they are trying to reduce their sodium intake.)

Rice Wine

Rice wine, also known as Shaoxing, is used in marinating and braising dishes. It has a flavor that is somewhat similar to dry sherry in flavor. In order to speed up the dispersion of alcohol and improve flavor, it is poured around the rim of the wok while stir-frying. It is also used in sauces and marinades, where it is combined with soy sauce and spices.

Sake and dry sherry are acceptable substitutes. To make mirin, use a teaspoon of sugar for every tablespoon of mirin used in the recipe.

COOKING METHODS

When it comes to cooking, Chinese cuisine employs a variety of techniques. Chinese chefs strive to keep food as fresh as possible while preserving its color, nutrients, and texture. Takeout recipes make more extensive use of frying than traditional recipes. Even though it is done in a wok, frying is not a common cooking method in traditional Chinese cuisine. Breading is another technique that has its origins in the United States. But Americanized dishes are evolving, and westerners are becoming more adventurous in their culinary explorations. The use of traditional cooking methods and the serving of more authentic dishes are no longer a source of concern for many Chinese restaurants.

Stir-Fry

This cooking method became popular in America because it is a quick, low-fat, and nutrient-preserving method. It involves cooking thinly sliced meat (sometimes pre-cooked) and vegetables with a soy sauce-based marinade. These are cooked in an ultra-hot wok with minimal oil and frequent stirring. The result is a hot, fresh dish of crisp and tasty ingredients. Large woks are preferred for better distribution of heat and more desirable texture and flavor. The key to stir-frying is to start with a very hot wok before adding oil.

Steaming

Chinese ingenuity and innovation are well-represented by this time, space, and fuel-saving cooking method. The steamer is made up of bamboo baskets stacked one on top of the other in about 3 layers. Several kinds of food can be cooked at a time over slow-boiling water. Popular steamed dishes are dim sums, such as buns or dumplings, pancakes, and fish.

Red Stewing

The name is taken from the resulting rich, brown color of the dishes using this cooking method. Unlike stir-fry, which uses the least amount of cooking time possible, this method requires several hours of cooking. Meats are usually seared first and cooked with soy sauce, rice wine, and traditional spices until tender and tasty.

Roasting

Large pieces of meat or whole chicken and duck are roasted in ovens. These are then chopped or sliced thinly and are usually served with a thick sauce or gravy.

Boiling

Commonly used for vegetables are boiled quickly, drained, and then served with a thick sauce. Noodles and soups are also cooked using this method.

Poaching

Fish are often cooked using this method. A tasty broth is used to impart flavor.

Deep Frying

This method is said to be more popular in Americanized recipes rather than in traditional cooking. The resulting dishes are crisp and tasty.

Tools for Cooking Chinese Food :

The basic tools are more or less the same as those found in any regular kitchen. Here are some useful tools that will give your cooking fun and authentic feel.

Wok

What is Chinese cooking without a wok? The wok is versatile and can be used for stir-frying, boiling, steaming, and deep-frying. Its rounded bottom results in a more efficient use of heat. Chefs prefer large woks for more efficient heat distribution and better results in terms of texture and flavor.

Rice Cooker

This is a very useful item for Chinese cooking. It does away with the need to constantly watch the rice cooking in a clay pot and gives you time to make other preparations. The rice cooker can also be used for boiling and steaming.

Steamer

The traditional steamer makes use of tiers of bamboo baskets, but modem designs can be metal. This is used for dim sum and fish dishes.

Cleaver

A large knife is used for cutting, slicing, and chopping. The flat side doubles as a smasher or crusher for garlic, ginger, and peppercorns.

Chopsticks

Chopsticks are indispensable to the Chinese cook. They can pick up ingredients, loosen noodle strands, mix, flip, and measure powdered ingredients. The chopsticks for cooking are made of bamboo or wood and are longer than regular ones.

Chinese Scissors

These make cutting much easier and faster than using knives. They can be used for meats, poultry, seafood, vegetables, and herbs.

Spider Strainer

This tool is used for scooping and straining at the same time. It has a web¬shaped mesh and is ideal for freshly-boiled noodles and deep-fried rolls, chicken, or seafood.

Because I come from an architectural background, I enjoy delving into the details of how each component of a recipe interacts with the others. Understanding why and how different ingredients interact with one another helps me figure out how to make the best bread, cookie, and cake possible. This section contains an explanation of the standard ingredients I use in my recipes and information on why, how, and when to use each one. It should be noted that the majority of the recipes in this book use common ingredients that most home cooks and bakers already have on hand or can easily obtain from their local supermarket.

FLOUR

Many of the recipes in this book are built around the use of flour. Each flour variety has its own set of inherent properties that contribute to creating a successful baked good. The type of flour specified in each recipe is deliberate, and it cannot be substituted for another without causing a significant reduction in the quality of the final product.

Bread flour is a wheat-based flour that contains a high amount of protein (11 to 14 percent). A higher protein content results in more gluten production, which gives bread its chewiness and structural strength. The higher absorption rate makes it an excellent choice for bread that requires a lot of milk, butter, and eggs to be baked into them.

All-purpose flour is another wheat-based flour with a lower protein content (9 to 10%) than bread flour. It is used in baking and cooking. Dumpling dough, green onion pancakes, puff pastry, steamed buns, and cookies are excellent uses for this flour. As the name implies, it can be used in virtually any recipe.

Cake flour has a low protein content (between 7 and 8 percent), which makes it ideal for light sponge cakes and souffles, which are made with it. I also prefer to use cake flour in my waffles and crepes because the batter hydrates much better and has a more delectable texture due to the higher moisture content.

Rice flour is made by finely milling rice grains into a fine powder. In terms of texture, depending on how you cook it, it can have crispy or chewy notes. Rice flour is frequently used in the preparation of bouncy rice noodles and the breading of crispy fried tofu. When combined with water, it produces a batter that can be used to make a White Sugar Cake and a Turnip Cake that can be used to hold savory bits of Chinese sausage and green onions in suspension. To get the best results in the recipes in this book, I recommend buying rice flour from Asian markets rather than American supermarkets because the rice flour from Asian markets tends to have a finer, almost powdery consistency that works better in the recipes than rice flour from American supermarkets that are sold in the "alternative ingredients" section.

Glutinous rice flour is made by milling short-grain sticky rice, which is a type of sticky rice. It behaves very differently from regular rice flour, and it is sometimes referred to as "mochiko" or "sweet rice flour" because of its sweetness. Glutinous rice flour is used as the foundation for Japanese mochi and other chewy treats like kakigori. Koda Farms is my preferred brand because it consistently produces the best and most consistent outcomes.

SUGAR

Granulated sugar is white cane sugar with a neutral sweetness that comes from cane sugar. The obvious benefit is that it sweetens recipes, but it also aids in the spreading of cookies in the oven, the incorporation of air into butter and egg whites, and the caramelization of sugar into beautiful shades of amber. Like every other ingredient in this book, the amount of sugar specified is intended to be used; therefore, resist the temptation to reduce the amount of sugar specified because you think it might be a little too sweet—trust me, it isn't.

It is cane sugar that has been combined with molasses to form brown sugar. I prefer dark brown sugar because of its darker color and stronger flavor, but light brown sugar can be used to substitute and tastes just as good. You want to make sure that the brown sugar is packed tightly into the measuring cup when you're measuring it.

DAIRY AND EGGS

When a recipe calls for milk, I typically use whole milk instead of skim milk. 2 percent, on the other hand, is usually sufficient as a substitute. Because of the low-fat content of skim or 1 percent milk, it should not be used in recipes. For the recipe to be successful, it must have a higher fat content.

Heavy cream is required for whipped creams, and it is also my preferred liquid for egg washes because the fat from the heavy cream caramelizes into a beautiful dark brown color in the oven, giving the finished product a luxurious appearance.

The water content of evaporated milk is approximately 60% lower than that of regular milk. It is available in cans, and even though it appears to be a somewhat dated baking ingredient, it is still widely used in Chinese bakeries and cafes. As a result of the evaporation process, it has an inherent caramelized flavor and extra-silky texture, making it essential for Hong Kong Milk Tea and enhancing the caramel flavors in Malay Cake.

The terms sweetened condensed milk and evaporated milk are frequently used interchangeably. It has also had approximately 60% of its water content removed, but it has been sweetened with sugar. As a result, you'll have a rich, super creamy, and extremely sweet mixture on your hands. When I see an opportunity to drizzle it onto something, I take advantage of it.

Coconut milk is produced by pressing the pulp of mature coconuts into a liquid form. It has a strong coconut flavor and is rich and creamy in texture. Only full-fat coconut milk should ever be purchased; avoid any coconut milk that is labeled as "lite" or "reduced fat," as well as any that contains additives (the only ingredients listed on the label should be coconut and water). Aroy-D and Chaokoh are two of my favorite brands, and they can usually be found in Asian grocery stores.

Unsalted butter should be used for baking purposes. Occasionally, I'll use salted butter when I'm sandwiching a patty inside a warm pineapple bun or spreading it over a piece of bread, but I won't use salted butter when baking. When you use unsalted butter in a recipe, you have complete control over how much salt is added. Temperature is also critical to the success of a recipe; some call for chilled, softened, or melted butter, while others call for chilled, softened, or melted butter. Allowing your butter to soften at room temperature ahead of time (an hour or so in a warm spot is a good general rule) is preferable to attempting to soften it in the microwave at the last minute. Once the butter has melted, it will not behave in the same way again, even if you allow it to firm back up again afterward.

Eggs should always be large and fresh, regardless of the season. Keeping large eggs in mind, the following recipes have been created. Make sure to save the gorgeous heirloom eggs for brunch.

OIL

Canola oil is what I reach for again and again in the kitchen. It is often used to create crispier and more supple bread, brushed onto cutting boards and in between layers of dough for thin and flaky pancakes, and added to cakes for moisture. In most baking sce¬narios, stick with canola oil or another neutral-flavored oil, like vegetable or grapeseed, so it doesn't interfere with the flavors of your bake. Reserve more robust olive oil for savory cooking or dipping crusty bread in.

Sesame oil is nutty and aromatic. It's one of my favorite ingredi¬ents to incorporate into marinades, sauces, dressings, and dumpling fillings. A little sesame oil goes a long way in flavoring your food.

OTHER

Yeast is a nonchemical leavening agent (as opposed to baking soda or baking powder) that aids in the rising of baked goods. The most widely available types of yeast are active dry yeast and instant yeast, both of which are available in large quantities. In contrast to active dry yeast, which must be activated in warm water or a liquid before being combined with other ingredients, instant yeast can be added directly to dry ingredients without the need for any prior activation. In the majority of cases, different types of yeast can be substituted without causing any issues. I typically use active dry yeast because, when mixed with water and sugar (a process known as "proofing"), you can see bubbles forming, indicating that the yeast is still alive and well and working properly. However, every now and then, a recipe (such as the steamed bun dough) will call for instant yeast because it performs better for that particular method and recipe.

Instead of individual packets of yeast, I prefer to purchase jars of yeast (both active dry, and instant) and keep them refrigerated to ensure freshness. I've been let down several times by yeast packets that have gone bad well before their expiration date. If your yeast isn't doing its job, you could end up wasting an entire batch of bread.

Salt is available in a variety of shapes and sizes. For cooking, I only use coarse salt, specifically Diamond Crystal kosher salt, available in bulk. The large, coarse grains dissolve in a short period. To avoid the risk of oversalting when using table salt instead of sea salt, use a little less than the recipe calls for to avoid the risk of oversalting when using sea salt instead of table salt (more grains of table salt can fit into a measuring spoon than the coarser kosher salt grains). Keep flaky sea salt on hand for finishing touches, such as sprinkling over a batch of salty-sweet cookies or sprinkling on top of warm buttery rolls.

White pepper predominates in my cooking over black pepper, which I believe is because I have spent my entire life watching my mother cook with it. The use of white pepper is more common in Chinese cooking than the use of black pepper. It's a little spicier, and it's also been ground into a fine powder, which allows it to become extremely airborne when you sprinkle it on top of something. (Whenever I use white pepper in my cooking, I sneeze a lot.)

Cornstarch is a common ingredient in Cantonese cuisine. A common application for this ingredient is as a sauce thickener in glossy stir-fries, in marinades to help tenderize tough cuts of meat, and in batters for fried foods to produce extra-crunchy coatings on the outside. Cornstarch is used in baking as a stabilizer and thickener, among other things. Cakes have a more tender crumb, and custards have a thick and creamy consistency because of the addition of this ingredient.

ESSENTIAL TYPOLOGIES

The term "Chinese bakery" can be very specific, but it's also broad in the sense that several different establishments provide bakery fare. Of course, some bakeries and cafes fall between these types because, like buns, each one is unique.

GRAB AND GO

This is the most common style of Chinese bakery in the United States. There are rows and rows of acrylic display cases crammed with every kind of bun and pastry you can imagine. Take out a cafeteria tray and a pair of tongs and begin browsing through the cases as soon as possible. With each one you walk past, you gradually fill up your tray until it is either time to check out or you can no longer carry anymore.

SPECIALTY SHOPS

Instead of offering a wide range of products, some bakeries specialize in only one or a small number of products. A specialty bakery could specialize in elaborately decorated fruit and cream cakes or offer the best cocktail bun in the city. It could also be open for only a few months out of the year, perhaps producing mooncakes for the Mid-Autumn Festival, or it could be open all year.

TAKEAWAY

Takeaway restaurants are hybrids of bakeries and dim sum par¬lors. My favorites in San Francisco are Good Luck Dim Sum and Xiao Long Bao, both on Clement Street. In the mornings, it's worth waiting in the long lines for your pick of steamed buns, flaky egg tarts, juicy soup dumplings, and noodles, all sold in a tight space.

SIT-DOWN CAFES

These often-bustling cafes take their inspiration from cha chaan things or Hong Kong-style diners and offer a warm pastry and a cup of tea for customers to enjoy. Menus at upscale bakeries and takeaway restaurants are typically more extensive than traditional bakeries and takeaway restaurants.

SHOPPING AT AN ASIAN GROCERY STORE

If you want to broaden your culinary horizons in Asian cuisine, becoming familiar with the products available at your local Asian grocery store is essential.

For those of you who live near an Asian grocery store but have been intimidated by the unfamiliar food items (or perhaps have been too intimidated to even walk into the store!), this guide will help you navigate your way through the store. Some helpful hints on how to navigate your local Asian grocery store with confidence will be shared in this article.

Even though you may find some useful information that applies to supermarkets in Asian countries, this article is geared toward shopping at Asian grocery stores in Western countries such as the United States, the United Kingdom, and others.

The foods and cuisines of various Asian countries such as China, India, Malaysia, Japan, Korea, Vietnam, and the Philippines can be sampled at an Asian grocery store by visiting one of their locations. What a fantastic way to expand your culinary horizons!

Furthermore, you may discover that the prices at some Asian supermarkets are lower than the prices at your local supermarkets! When comparing prices between different supermarkets, I've discovered that vegetables, in particular, are frequently less expensive.

VISITING AN ASIAN GROCERY STORE IN YOUR NEIGHBORHOOD

Your neighborhood may have more than one Asian grocery store. I recommend going to as many as you can to get a better sense of what they have to offer, how their store is laid out, and so on. Find one or two stores where you feel most comfortable shopping and stick with them. Keep in mind that some stores may specialize in foods from specific regions, such as Japan or Korea, and that you may not be able to find certain items from other countries, such as India, in these stores.

It certainly helps to be prepared when shopping at a traditional grocery store, just as it does at any other type of store. Plan your meals ahead of time so that you know exactly what you'll need for your shopping list when you get there.

Either print out the recipe (preferably along with a photo) and bring it with you to the Asian grocery store or have the recipe and photo-ready on your phone before you leave home for the trip. Suppose you require assistance in locating any ingredients. In that case, you can approach any store employee or even the store owner for assistance. They are usually more than happy and willing to help you out with whatever you need.

Using a translation app such as Google Translate to communicate with a store employee or owner if a language barrier is recommended.

Show them the recipe as well as a photograph of the dish that you intend to prepare (either from a printout or from your phone), if possible. They may even be able to provide you with some helpful hints and pointers when it comes to preparing the dish! When I've asked the store owner about specific products, he's been able to tell me which brands of those products are most frequently purchased by local restaurants.

The ingredients or instructions on the label or packaging of some items at the Asian grocery store may not be English, so check the label or packaging before purchasing. The Google Translate app on your phone can "read" characters in certain languages, such as Chinese and Korean, and display the English translation right on the image!

Of course, the translation is not always going to be 100 percent accurate (and can be downright hilarious at times!), but it will at the very least provide you with a general idea of what is being said.

Even though every Asian grocery store has a unique layout, the following is a general overview of the sections that you would typically find in an Asian grocery store:

DIFFERENT TYPES OF RICE

Given that rice is a staple in almost all Asian cuisines, it should come as no surprise that you will find an enormous variety of rice in any Asian supermarket.

When cooked, short-grain rice has a slightly sticky and starchy texture, similar to brown rice. Short grain rice is commonly used in sushi, and I enjoy making congee out of it.

When cooked, medium-grain rice is a little more fluffy than long-grain rice. It has a moist and tender texture. The majority of varieties of Jasmine rice, which is probably one of the most popular types of rice for Asian cooking (and my personal favorite), are considered medium to long-grained in texture. Rice with a delicate texture and aroma, such as jasmine, accompanies most Asian dishes.

Long grain rice is chewier and separates much more easily than medium and short-grain rice, and it is also more expensive. Basmati rice is a popular example of a long-grain rice variety.

Glutinous rice is also very popular in a lot of Asian cooking, so when purchasing any type of rice from an Asian grocery store, always double-check the label to make sure that you are purchasing the correct type of rice, as both types of rice appear to be very similar to each other in appearance.

Please see the following step-by-step guides if you would like to learn how to cook rice without the use of a rice cooker:

DIFFERENT TYPES OF NOODLE

A staple of Asian cuisine, noodles are also a staple of the American diet. In most Asian grocery stores, entire aisles are dedicated to different types of (dried) noodles. Rice noodles, egg noodles, and several other types of noodles and a variety of sizes and thicknesses are available for purchase.

The type of noodle you purchase will be determined by the dish you are preparing in your kitchen. Generally, the type of noodle used in a recipe is not interchangeable, so it is best to stick with the type specified in the recipe.

Here are some examples of common noodles and the applications for which they are used:

- Pad See Ew (also known as Beef Chow Fun) is an extra-wide rice noodle.

- Pad Thai is a type of wide rice noodle.
- Fried Rice Vermicelli is a thin rice noodle (also known as vermicelli) (by Rasa Malaysia)
- Pad Thai with bean thread noodle (glass noodle): Woon Sen Wonton Noodles are also known as Dry Wonton Noodles (by What to Eat Today)
- Yellow noodles (e.g., Yakisoba): Indonesian Mie Goreng (yellow noodle soup).
- Traditional Shoyu Ramen is a type of Japanese Ramen noodle.
- Kitsune Udon is a type of Japanese udon noodle (by Just One Cookbook)
- Zaru Soba (buckwheat noodles) is a type of Japanese soba noodle.

What's great about buying dried noodles is that they'll last a very long time in your pantry if you store them properly. Because they are so inexpensive, you can buy them in bulk and store them until you need them, saving you money.

Apart from dried noodles, fresh noodles are also readily available in the refrigerated section of most Asian supermarkets. Fresh noodles have a much shorter shelf life when compared to dried noodles, so you will want to use them as soon as possible after preparing the dish.

Most of the time, the noodle (or rice) aisle is where you'll find rice paper, which is necessary for making Vietnamese spring rolls.

FRUITS AND VEGETABLES

Asian supermarkets have a fantastic selection of fruits and vegetables, which I find to be particularly appealing. There are a plethora of options, all of which are usually extremely fresh. When I buy bean sprouts, I always buy them from an Asian grocery store because they are often much fresher and crisper than at the supermarket.

In addition to the vegetables typically found in Asian dishes, you will also see some vegetables that are very familiar to you and that you would find at your local grocery store; most of the time, they are less expensive than the Asian vegetables!

Adding more fruits and vegetables to our diets is something we all know we should do, and shopping for produce at your local Asian grocery store is a fantastic way to discover new and delicious varieties. Don't be afraid to try new things; you might just discover your new favorite recipe!

Fruits to try include:

- Mangoes de Rambutan (Rambutan Mangoes) (various types)
- Lychees
- Jackfruit

Recipes for Mangosteen Vegetables include:

- The root of the lotus
- Choy Sum Kai Lan (Choy Sum Kai Lan) (Chinese broccoli)
- Bok Choy Mustard Greens (also known as Bok Choy)

SEAFOOD

Fresh or even live seafood may be available in larger Asian supermarkets, whereas smaller Asian markets will typically keep their seafood in the frozen section.

Given that some cultures prefer to cook their fish whole (for example, Chinese cuisine), you will frequently find a wide variety of whole fish for sale.

In addition to sushi-grade raw fish, fish roe, crab sticks, and other ingredients for making your own sushi, you can find them in this frozen seafood section.

SAUCE AND SEASONING

A trip down the sauce aisle at an Asian supermarket can be intimidating due to the many different types of sauces available and the numerous different brands available. When it comes to Asian cooking, the truth is that you only need a handful of the most commonly used sauces in your pantry.

In my kitchen, I always have a few sauces available (remember that I cook a lot of Asian foods, so this list can be considered quite extensive): <u>Here are some of the sauces that I keep on hand:</u>

- Soy sauce (in a light version)
- Soy sauce in a dark color
- Oyster sauce is a sauce made from oysters.
- Hoisin sauce is a type of sauce that comes from Japan.
- Fish sauce is a type of sauce that is made from fish.
- Rice vinegar is a type of vinegar that is made from rice.
- Shaoxing wine is a type of Chinese medicine.
- Mirin is a type of sesame oil.
- Sriracha chili sauce is a type of hot sauce.
- Thai chili sauce (also known as thai chili sauce)

Build your collection from the ground up, starting with a good soy sauce, oyster sauce, and Shaoxing wine as a foundation, and expanding your collection as you cook more and more Asian recipes.

Other sauces on the shelves are usually pre-mixed/prepared, such as teriyaki sauce, which you can easily make at home using the other sauces you already have in your pantry.

In addition to sauces, you will often find a variety of dried spices and pastes alongside the sauces (such as curry pastes). You can even find pre-mixed pastes, sauces, and spices for specific dishes in packets that have already been mixed. In most cases, all that is required is the addition of meats and vegetables, which can be accomplished by simply following the instructions on the package. If you want to try those dishes at home, this is a very convenient option.

FROZEN FOOD

For this reason, Asian supermarkets tend to import many food items from other countries, so their frozen and refrigerated sections are typically very large to keep those foods fresh.

Fresh meats, miso pastes, fresh chili pastes, kimchi, fresh noodles, and various other items can be found in the refrigerator section.

Some cuts of meat that aren't as popular in Western cuisine, such as pork belly and short ribs, as well as thinly sliced meats for Japanese shabu-shabu, can be found in this section.

There are some really interesting foods in the frozen food section, such as frozen dim sum, that you should check out. You might even come across some frozen produce! This is especially useful because some imported vegetables and fruits do not last very long in the refrigerator but can last for months in the freezer if properly stored.

Some of the items I frequently purchase from this section include frozen minced lemongrass (which is so convenient!!), frozen Thai bird chili, frozen banana leaf (which is used to serve dishes such as Penang Char Koay Teow), frozen kaffir lime leaves, and frozen curry leaves, to name a few. These items are very common in Asia, but they are much more difficult to come by in Western countries, making it convenient to have them on hand in your freezer.

SNACKS AND BEVERAGES

They particularly enjoy exploring the snack and beverage sections of the Asian grocery store when my husband and children accompany me there. In addition, it happens to be one of my favorite sections... In fact, I rarely leave the store without at least one or two snack items in my shopping cart!)

There are a plethora of different snacks to choose from. If you're not familiar with this type of cuisine, some dishes can be intimidating (whole crispy anchovies, anyone? (How about some smoked ham floss?) However, a large number of them are quite delicious.

Although shrimp crackers may appear to be a strange combination, they are one of our favorites.

The beverage section is chock-full of intriguing and exotic flavors to try. Roasted coconut juice is a personal favorite of ours.

KITCHEN UTENSILS

You will find a large selection of woks, wok spatulas, ladles, frying pans, and other kitchen and household items in the kitchen and household section. All of the kitchen equipment you'll need to prepare (and serve) Asian cuisine in your own home!

If you are new to Asian cooking, I have compiled a list of the Top 10 Asian Kitchen Essentials that you can refer to for further guidance and inspiration. Your local Asian grocery store should have many of these items, if not all, of the items on this shopping list.

ESSENTIAL EQUIPMENT FOR CHINESE BAKING

Start with this list of baking tool essentials if you're a beginner baker who's just getting started (or a master chef who wants to declutter their workspace). We'll assist you in putting together a baking essentials kit for beginners, which includes 21 pastry tools.

Beginner bakers and seasoned professionals are invited to join us. It is possible to organize your baking equipment once and for all with the help of this list of baking supplies. Beginners should start with our list of must-have baking equipment to equip their kitchens with all of the essential baking tools they'll need to complete any sweet treat recipe they come across. In addition, if you are attempting to perfect a cake recipe or a more difficult pastry recipe, be sure to check out our list of must-have baking tools to begin stocking your kitchen with equipment that will make your process faster, easier and more impressive.

These are the tools that you absolutely must-have in your kitchen, and they're the ones that you'll use far more frequently than you realize. Make sure you have these tools on hand before you begin baking a cake or mixing up a batch of cookies.

Precision is essential when baking, which is why having a complete set of measuring cups and spoons on hand is essential. Never assume that you can get by with just one type of measuring cup; you will need both dry and wet measuring cups to accurately measure all of your ingredients in the kitchen. Keep these tools in an easy-to-reach location because you'll be using them regularly.

Most measuring spoon sets include a tablespoon, a teaspoon, a 12 teaspoon, and a 14 teaspoon, while most measuring cups are available in sets of one cup, one cup and a half, one cup and a third, and one cup and a fourth. One-cup measuring cups are sufficient for liquid measurements, but having two- and four-cup sizes in your cupboard can also be useful.

Wooden Spoons

One wooden spoon is sufficient, but because this tool is so useful, it can be beneficial to have a couple on hand at all times. In addition to being extremely durable (you will be able to use them with even the thickest and heaviest doughs), wooden spoons are excellent for all types of stirring. Just make sure to hand-wash them after you're finished to avoid them becoming cracked or discolored.

Rubber Spatula/Scaper

We're willing to bet that you reach for your rubber scraper a lot more frequently than you realize. Using this tool, you can scrape the last bit of batter or dough out of a pan or scrape all of the nooks and crannies out of a jam jar, which is particularly useful when baking. They're also extremely useful for mixing wet and dry ingredients together. Scrapers made of silicone will fare better in high temperatures than scrapers made of rubber.

Metal Spatula

When it comes to transferring freshly baked cookies to a cooling rack or serving a piece of cake from a 9x13 pan, there's no better tool than a good old spatula to do the job. Being able to use one with a thin metal blade can be particularly useful, as it will be flexible enough to easily slide under

20

whatever you're moving without squishing the dough or crumbling your cookies, which is ideal.

Pastry Brushes

You may not have realized how many applications this handy tool has. In addition to preparing cake batter, it can be used to coat the dough with melted butter or egg wash and "paint" milk on top of a pie crust, among other things. This is an absolute must-have, especially if you bake regularly!

Whisk

Sure, a wire whisk can be used to whisk together a few eggs, but it can also be used for various other tasks. Furthermore, it is one of the most effective methods for thoroughly mixing dry ingredients, and it is also excellent for stirring together a homemade custard mixture.

Scissors

We always have our kitchen shears on hand when we're preparing a recipe, whether it's for baking or otherwise. In various situations, they can be extremely useful, including snipping fresh herbs, cutting the parchment paper to fit a pan, and even simply opening stubborn packages and containers.

Pincers (Rolling Pins)

Rolling pins are unquestionably the most useful tool in the kitchen for rolling out pie crusts, cookie dough, and puff pastry, but there are a variety of other uses for this tool in the kitchen. For example, if you don't have a food processor and need to crush cookies, chips, or crackers for a recipe, simply place them in a sealable bag and smash them with a rolling pin until they are crumbled.

Sieve with a Fine Mesh

A sieve can be put to use in a variety of different applications. Baking enthusiasts will probably find this device to be of greatest assistance when sieving dry ingredients or dusting powdered sugar onto a finished pan of brownies or cookies. The baking tool is also useful for draining wet ingredients (especially small ones, such as quinoa that would slip through a regular colander) and removing seeds from raspberry sauces, among other things.

Chef's Knife

If you only have one knife in your entire kitchen, make it this one. It will serve you well. This all-purpose knife is ideal for slicing, dicing, chopping, and mincing just about any ingredient that your recipe calls for. It is dishwasher safe.

Paring Knife

Yes, you want this knife to be a part of your knife collection. It's particularly useful for peeling and coring foods such as apples. Besides cutting up other fruits and vegetables, it can also be used for more delicate tasks that your chef's knife is too large to handle properly.

Baking Pan with a Rectangular Shape

A standard baking pan (13x9x2 inches) is an absolute must-have for any baker. You can use it in a variety of sweet recipes, such as cakes, brownies, and cookie bars, and, of course, it has savory applications as well. If you only have one baking pan in your kitchen, make it this one. It will serve you well.

A Round Cake Pan

To be completely honest, you should have two of these baking supplies on hand because you'll need more than one to create a stunning layer of cake. Round cake pans are available in two sizes: 8-inch and 9-inch in diameter; however, most layer cake recipes can be made with either size (just make sure you have two of the same size).

Pan for Making Loaf

A loaf pan is required for all of our favorite homemade bread recipes, whether it's banana bread, pumpkin bread, or zucchini bread. If you want to make your own yeast bread, it will be beneficial to have two of these pans in your kitchen cabinet.

Pie Plate

Though the most obvious use for a pie plate is for baking your own homemade pies, there are a variety of other desserts that make having this baking item handy. In addition, you can make savory pies for dinner, such as meatball pie or taco pie, as well as frozen icebox pies for the freezer. They're also great for shallow dishes when dredging and breading meats and poultry.

Square Baking Pan

You don't always need to make a large batch of brownies, and if you only want to make a small batch, a square baking pan will suffice. A few of the baked goods made with this baking accessory include cookie bars, cakes, brownies, and corn bread.

Wire Organizer

Make sure you have a wire rack in your kitchen for baking cookies and cakes because no one wants soggy, overbaked cookies and cakes for dessert. This useful tool allows air to circulate around baked goods as they cool, ensuring that they taste just as good at room temperature as they did when they were first taken out of the oven.

Muffin Pan

Bring a tray of freshly baked muffins to your next brunch, or use it to make birthday cupcakes for your friends and family to share. In addition, a muffin pan can be used for a variety of savory recipes, such as meatballs, pizza cups, and mini meat loaves, among others.

Baking/Cookie/Sheet Pan

Cookie sheets are a must-have in any kitchen, and having two will almost certainly be more convenient than having one. If you decide to use two cookie sheets, we recommend using one cookie sheet with one raised side to bake your cookies. This will allow for proper air circulation and even the baking of your cookies. However, baking sheets and sheet pans with raised sides can also be used for cookies, and they are the best choice for sheet pan dinner recipes.

Hand/Stand Mixers

While you are not required to purchase a high-end stand mixer, you should have at the very least a hand mixer in your collection of baking tools. It makes mixing up doughs and batters much easier and faster, and it's by far the most effective way to combine ingredients into a thick, stiff cookie dough without tiring out your arm and wrist.

Parchment Paper

If you haven't been baking with parchment paper yet, now is the time to start. Preparing your pan by spreading a sheet of parchment paper over it before baking cookies will make cleanup much easier and prevent your baked goods from sticking to the pan. Baking enthusiasts may want to consider purchasing a reusable silicone baking mat ($21, Target) to reduce their carbon footprint.

PART 2:
THE RECIPES

SWEET, SAVORY BAKED AND FRIED BUN

COOL PORK BELLY BUNS

Prep Time: 30 minutes + 1 Hour 20 Minutes Rise Time
Cooking Time: 120 minutes
Number of Servings: 10 Buns

Ingredients:

For Steamed Buns
- 3 tablespoon unsalted butter
- 1 tablespoon olive oil
- 2 teaspoon instant dried yeast
- 3 tablespoon whole milk
- 3 3/4 cups flour
- 1/2 teaspoon salt
- 3/4 cup warm water
- 2 tablespoon caster sugar

Slow-Cooked Pork Belly
- 1 tablespoon rice wine
- 1 tablespoon caster sugar
- 1 tablespoon minced ginger
- 3 cloves garlic
- 4 1/4 cups chicken stock
- 2.2 lb. rindless pork belly

Pork Belly Glaze
- 1 tablespoon vegetable oil 1 cup cold water
- 1 teaspoon black sesame seeds (for garnish)
- 1 teaspoon spring onions, finely chopped (for garnish)

For the vinegar dipping sauce
- 3 tablespoon dark soy sauce
- 1 teaspoon lemongrass paste
- 2 tablespoon honey
- 2 tablespoon brown sugar
- 2 tablespoon vegetable oil
- 1 tablespoon minced ginger
- 1 red chili
- 1 pinch of salt and pepper

Method:

1. Begin by preparing the bao buns.
2. In a mixing bowl, combine the flour, salt, sugar, and yeast.
3. Combine the milk, hot water, and butter in a jug and whisk until the butter has melted.
4. In an oiled pan, position the dough.
5. Begin preparing the pork belly in the meantime.
6. In a pan, combine all of the ingredients for the slow-cooked pork belly.
7. Re-knead the dough and divide it into ten balls.
8. Position the buns on the baking trays in the oven.
9. Place a large wok pan over high heat and bring to a boil.
10. Slice the pork into small bite-size pieces.
11. In a deep fryer, heat one tablespoon of the oil.
12. Add the oil and insert the pork, along with the salt and black pepper, to fry at medium temperature until the pork turns golden.
13. Cover the buns and fill them with a sticky pork belly once they have finished cooking. Sesame seeds should be sprinkled on top.

CRISPY SHANGAI PAN-FRIED PORK BUNS

Prep Time: 30 minutes + 1 Hour 20 Minutes Rise Time
Cooking Time: 120 minutes
Number of Servings: 15 Buns

Ingredients:

For the filling
- 200 grams ground pork
- 1/2 cup spring onions, finely chopped
- tablespoon fresh ginger, grated
- tablespoons soy sauce
- 1 teaspoon sesame oil
- 1 teaspoon Shaoxing cooking wine
- 1 teaspoon sugar
- 1 teaspoon white pepper
- 1 teaspoon black pepper (optional)

For the vinegar dipping sauce
- 2 tablespoons black vinegar
- 1/2 tablespoon soy sauce
- 1 teaspoon sesame oil
- 1 tablespoon green onions, finely chopped

For the bun dough
- 250 g all-purpose flour (2 cups)
- grams instant yeast (1 teaspoon)
- grams sugar (1 teaspoon)
- 4 grams baking powder (1 teaspoon)
- 150 grams water (150 ml)

For pan-frying the buns
- 1 tablespoon vegetable oil 1 cup cold water
- 1 teaspoon black sesame seeds (for garnish)
- 1 teaspoon spring onions, finely chopped (for garnish)

Method:

1. Combine all of the filling ingredients (ground pork, spring onions, ginger, soy sauce, sesame oil, cooking wine, sugar, white pepper, and black pepper) in a large mixing bowl (optional).
2. Mix the ingredients well and evenly with a spatula to allow the flavors to infuse into the ground meat.
3. Cover the bowl with plastic wrap and place in the refrigerator for at least one hour, or until the dough is ready to assemble.
4. In a large mixing bowl, combine the flour, yeast, sugar, baking powder, salt, and water. Using a spatula, combine the ingredients until they form a dough. Scrape down the sides of the bowl to remove any remaining dry flour.
5. Knead the dough with your hands (or a stand mixer) for about 10 minutes, or until it is smooth and soft. This dough has a water-to-flour ratio of 60% and should be fairly easy to handle.
6. Form the dough into a ball and return it to the bowl. Wrap a chopping board or cling wrap around the bowl. Allow the dough to rise and double in size at room temperature for one hour.
7. Once the dough has risen, knead it for a few minutes to remove any air bubbles.
8. Roll the dough into a log on a floured surface. Divide the log into 15 equal pieces and roll into balls by cupping them in your palm and rolling them in a circular motion. With a small rolling pin, flatten and roll each dough ball into a 3-inch circle. It is important to note that the center should be slightly thicker than the edges.

9. Fill the center of the rolled-out dough with a tablespoon of the filling.
10. Bring the dough's edges up, enclosing the filling inside.
11. Using your finger, pleat the edges together to seal the filling inside.
12. Place the buns on a parchment-lined tray or plate, pleated side up (the top side should be smooth). Cover with a tea towel and set aside for 20 minutes to allow the dough to rise even more (not double in size).
13. Heat the oil in a large skillet over medium-high heat for 2 minutes. Place the buns with the pleated side down. To prevent buns from sticking together, space them approximately V2 inches apart. (If your skillet is too small, you may need to cook in two batches.) Cook for another 2 minutes, or until the bottom is golden brown and crispy.
14. 1 cup of cold water should be added to the pan. The water should immediately begin to sizzle and bubble. Make sure the water is about V2-inch deep and covers half the height of the buns. Cook, covered, for 8-10 minutes, or until almost all of the water has evaporated.
15. Remove the lid and turn the heat down to medium. Cook for 2 minutes more, or until all of the water has been absorbed and the bottom is crispy brown. Top with sesame seeds and green onions.
16. Place the buns on a plate and repeat the process with the second batch.
17. Serve hot with a vinegar dipping sauce on the side.

AWESOME PINEAPPLE BUNS

Prep Time: 30 minutes + Rising Time
Cooking Time: 120 minutes
Number of Servings: 10 Buns

Ingredients:

For Dough Topping
- 1 egg yolk
- 1/2 teaspoon vanilla extract
- 1/4 cup vegetable shortening
- 2 tablespoons milk
- VA cup nonfat dry milk powder
- 1/4t easpoon baking powder
- 2/3 cup superfine sugar
- 1/2 teaspoon baking soda
- 1 and 1/4 cups all-purpose flour

To Finish
- 1 whole egg yolk

For Dough Bread
- 1 tablespoon active dry yeast
- 1 and 1/2 teaspoons salt
- 1/2 cup cake flour
- 3 and 1/2 cups bread flour
- 2/3 cup heavy cream
- 1 large egg
- 1/3 cup sugar
- 1 cup milk

Method:

1. Begin by making the dough for the bread.
2. Combine the dough components in the bucket of an electric mixer.
3. The dough is prepared for proofing after fifteen minutes.
4. Allow the buns to rise for the next hour under a clean, wet kitchen towel.
5. In a measuring dish, add the dry powdered milk.
6. Combine the flour, white vinegar, icing sugar, and superfine sugar in a large mixing bowl.
7. To mix, stir all together.
8. Combine the shortening, butter, egg yolk, and vanilla essence in a mixing bowl.
9. Heat the oven to 350 degrees F once the buns have finished growing a second time.
10. Divide the coating dough into 12 equal portions and roll each into a ball.
11. Rub with egg white and cook for 12 -13 minutes at 3 5 0 degrees.
12. Serve and enjoy once done!

CHINESE BAKED BBQ PORK BUNS (SIU BAO)

Prep Time: 4 Hours
Cooking Time: 25 minutes
Number of Servings: 8

Ingredients:

For Dough

- 2/3 gallon of heavy cream (at room temperature)
- 1 gallon of milk (whole milk preferred, but you can use 2 percent, at room temperature)
- 1 egg, large (at room temperature)
- 1/2 cup cake flour (can substitute 1/2 cup all-purpose flour sifted with 1 tablespoon cornstarch) 1/3 cup sugar
- a third and a half cup of bread flour (tap measuring cup to avoid air pockets)
- 1 tbsp. yeast (active dry) (or instant yeast)
- a half-teaspoon of salt

For Filling

- 2 tablespoons vegetable oil 1/2 cup finely chopped shallots (or onion) 2 tablespoons granulated sugar
- 2 teaspoons soy sauce (light)
- a couple of tablespoons of oyster sauce
- a teaspoon and a half of sesame oil
- 2 teaspoons soy sauce (dark)
- a third of a cup of chicken stock
- 2 tbsp. flour (all-purpose)
- 2 cups Chinese pork roast (char siu, finely diced)

For Finishing

- 1 tablespoon sesame seeds (optional)
- 1 tablespoon sesame seeds (optional)
- 1 tablespoon granulated sugar
- 1 egg wash (1 egg, beaten with 1 tablespoon water) (dissolved in 1 tablespoon boiling water)

Method:

1. Add the dough ingredients in the following order to the bowl of a stand mixer fitted with the dough hook attachment. Begin with the heavy cream, milk, and egg, all of which should be at room temperature. Then, add the sugar, cake flour, bread flour, yeast, and salt in that order.
2. To bring the dough together, turn the mixer to the lowest setting. Knead on low speed for 15 minutes once a scraggly dough has formed. If necessary, turn off the mixer and use a rubber spatula to bring the dough together. Alternatively, you can combine all of the dough ingredients in a large mixing bowl with a wooden spoon, then knead by hand for 20 minutes.
3. The dough should be able to stick to the bottom of the bowl but not the sides. If the dough sticks to the sides of the mixing bowl because you live in a humid climate, add more flour 1 tablespoon at a time until it comes together.
4. Cover the dough with an overturned plate or damp towel after shaping it into a ball. Place the dough in a warm place to proof for 75-90 minutes, or until it has doubled in size. (A closed microwave with a mug of hot boiled water next to the bowl is a good proofing environment.)
5. Make the meat filling while this is going on. To make the buns easier to fill, dice the pork finely rather than in large chunks. In a wok, heat 2 tablespoons of oil over medium heat. Stir-fry for 2 minutes with the shallot/onion. Combine the sugar,

28

soy sauce, oyster sauce, sesame oil, and dark soy sauce in a mixing bowl. Cook, constantly stirring until it begins to bubble. Combine the chicken stock and flour in a mixing bowl. Reduce the heat to low and cook, constantly stirring, for 2-3 minutes, or until the sauce has thickened. Add the roast pork and mix well.

6. Remove the filling from the wok onto a large plate after turning off the heat. To ensure an even amount of filling in each bun, divide the filling into 16 roughly equal piles. Allow cooling before serving.

7. Punch the air out of the dough for another 5 minutes after the first proof. Dump the dough onto a floured surface and roll it into a ball.

8. It should be cut into 16 equal pieces (in half, then quarters, then in quarters again). The best way to make sure your buns are all the same size is to weigh the entire dough ball, divide by 16, and then weigh each individual piece to match that weight.

9. Knead each individual dough ball to remove any air bubbles and smooth it out before shaping the buns. Roll it into a 4-inch circle, slightly thicker in the center than the edges.

10. Keep your hands clean while putting the buns together. Any grease from the filling on your fingers will make sealing them extremely difficult.

11. Fill the bun with 1 portion of the filling and crimp it shut, making sure it's tightly sealed. Place them 3 inches apart on baking sheets lined with parchment paper, seam side down.

12. Allow rising for another hour at room temperature, covered with a clean towel.

13. Preheat the oven to 400°F/200°C and place two racks in the top and bottom thirds. Brush the buns with egg wash and, if desired, sprinkle with sesame seeds.

14. Place the buns in the oven and reduce the temperature to 350°F/175°C right away. Preheat oven to 350°F and bake for 22-25 minutes, or until golden brown.

15. Remove the buns from the oven and brush them with the sugar syrup while they're still warm. Cool, and have fun!

PERFECT BAKED PORK BAO

Prep Time: 3 Hours
Cooking Time: 30 minutes
Number of Servings: 8

Ingredients:

For Dough
- 2 cups bread flour plus 1 tablespoon
- 2/3 cup flour (all-purpose)
- 2 tbsp. dry active yeast
- 2/3 cup sugar, granulated
- 1/4 cup vegetable shortening or lard (butter will also work)
- a single egg
- 3/4 cup plus 3 tablespoons of water (50 mL)

For Filling
- 1 cup of water
- 3/4 pound pork ground
- 1 teaspoon of sugar
- 2 tbsp soy sauce (optional)
- 1 teaspoon wine made from rice
- 1 tablespoon sauce (oyster)
- 1 tbsp hoisin sauce
- 1 teaspoon sesame oil, toasted
- 1 tbsp cornstarch, dissolved in 1 tbsp water

Method:

1. In a medium saucepan, whisk together 1 tablespoon flour and 3 tablespoons (50 milliliters) water until the flour is completely dissolved. Place the pan over medium heat and constantly stir for 3-5 minutes, or until the mixture resembles a thick paste. Place aside. This is the flour paste (tangzhong).
2. Combine the flour, sugar, salt, and yeast in a large mixing bowl. Combine the flour paste (tangzhong), 1 egg, and lard in a mixing bowl. Stir everything together to make a soft dough, then knead it for 15-20 minutes (by hand or with the dough hook attachment of your mixer). Form the dough into a ball and place it in a bowl that has been lightly greased. Allow rising for 1 hour, covered with a damp cloth.
3. In a small saucepan, brown the ground pork for the filling. If there is a lot of fat, drain it. Set aside the pork.
4. Combine the water, sugar, soy sauce, rice wine, oyster sauce, hoisin sauce, and sesame oil in a mixing bowl. Cook the sauce on medium heat until it begins to bubble. Cook for 1 minute, stirring, after adding the cornstarch mixture. Add ground pork to thicken the sauce significantly. Allow cooling to room temperature.
5. Cut the dough into 20 pieces that are all the same size. Take it one step at a time. Take one of the pieces and knead it into a round shape before pressing it flat. Work the edges of the dough circle thinner than the center of the circle, which you want to keep a little thicker.
6. Place a heaping teaspoon of the filling in the center of the circle. Pull the edges of the dough over the filling and pinch the dough together to seal the bun completely. Bring the edges together by gently pinching and twisting.
7. Set the buns aside on a floured or parchment-lined baking sheet. Make sure the side with the pinched seal is on the bottom. Repeat with the remaining 20 pieces until you have 20 buns.
8. Set the buns aside for 30 minutes to allow the dough to ferment further. Preheat your oven to 350°F at this time.
9. Brush the surface of each bun with some of the egg wash before placing them in the

oven (beaten egg plus 1 tablespoon of water). Bake for 20-25 minutes, or until the top is golden brown. To test for doneness, cut one of the buns in half and see if the bread is baked all the way through or still doughy.

10. You can eat a couple of these right away, but if you want to save them, place them in the fridge or freezer. Warm them up at 350°F for 5-10 minutes if reheating from the fridge. Allow them to defrost if they come from the freezer.

THE PERFECT BAKED HOISIN CHICKEN BUN

Prep Time: 4 Hours
Cooking Time: 25 minutes
Number of Servings: 9

Ingredients:

- Spray cooking oil
- 12 oz. skinless and boneless chicken thighs
- 14 cup finely diced green onions
- 1 12 tbsp. hoisin sauce
- 1 teaspoon oyster sauce
- 2 tablespoons rice vinegar
- 9 thawed frozen white roll dough pieces (such as Rich's)
- 1 large, lightly beaten egg
- 1 teaspoon toasted sesame seeds

Method:

1. Melt butter in a nonstick skillet over medium-high heat. Spray the pan with cooking spray. Cook for 4 minutes on each side, or until chicken is done. Allow cooling slightly before shredding the meat with two forks. In a medium mixing bowl, combine the chicken. Toss in the green onions, hoisin sauce, oyster sauce, and vinegar to combine.
2. On a lightly floured surface, roll each dough piece into a 4-inch circle. Fill each dough circle with about 2 tablespoons of the chicken mixture. Gather the dough's edges over the filling and pinch to seal. Place the filled dough on a baking sheet sprayed with cooking spray, seam sides down. Coat the filled dough lightly with cooking spray. Allow rising for 20 minutes, covered.
3. Preheat the oven to 375° F.
4. Unwrap the filled dough. Brush gently with egg; discard the remaining egg. Sesame seeds should be evenly distributed. Bake for 15 minutes at 375°F, or until golden brown. Serve hot.

HOMEY BAKED BAO BUNS WITH STEAK FILLING

Prep Time: 3 Hours
Cooking Time: 25 minutes
Number of Servings: 12

Ingredients:

- 3 cups maida (All purpose flour)
- 2 teaspoon yeast
- 2 teaspoon baking powder
- 3 tablespoons oil
- 1 tablespoon butter 1 teaspoon salt
- 1 teaspoon sugar, as needed Warm milk (for binding)

For Pickles

- 1/2 Cucumber (juliennes)
- a half carrot (grated)
- 1 onion, sliced
- 1 cayenne pepper (jullienes)
- 1 green pepper (chopped)
- 4 tablespoons Vinegar pinch salt

Filling for a steak

1. Fillet (1/2 kg) (Chinese cut)
2. 1 teaspoon salt
3. 1 teaspoon of black pepper powder
4. 1 teaspoon chili flakes
5. 12 cup lemon juice
6. 1 teaspoon garlic (pounded)
7. 1 teaspoon ginger (pounded)
8. 1/2 teaspoon Soy sauce
9. 1 tablespoon sugar (optional)
10. 1 teaspoon cornflour (mixed in 4 tbsp water)

Method:

1. To make the buns, combine the dry ingredients, add the oil and butter and combine thoroughly.
2. Bind with warm milk to form a soft dough, knead thoroughly, and set aside to rise.
3. Punch back and form twelve balls, then roll each into a one-centimeter thick on long puri when finished.
4. Place a piece of foil halfway down the puri (semicircle), then bring the remaining puri on top of the foil as if you were making a semicircle, or simply brush with oil all over the puri and fold in half.
5. Place each semicircle puri on a greased tray, leaving a few centimeters between them.
6. Glaze with a beaten egg Sprinkle with sesame seeds (optional) and allow to rise completely.
7. Bake at 340 degrees F until the top is nicely browned.
8. Typically, bao buns are steamed.
9. Make the pickles: Put all vegetables in a bowl, add the vinegar and salt, and mix well. Set aside.
10. Make the filling: Place the steak in a bowl with the remaining ingredients, except the cornflour mixture, and marinate for three hours.
11. Pour four tablespoons of oil into a nonstick pan and keep the heat on high.
12. Fry the marinated fillet until it is browned.
13. Toss well and remove from the heat after adding the cornflour mixture, which tends to form lumps.
14. Stuff the buns with fried fillets and pickles.

AUTHENTIC CHINESE BAKED BUNS

Prep Time: 30 minutes
Cooking Time: 30 minutes
Number of Servings: 4

Ingredients:

For Filling
- 2 cups diced roast chicken meat
- 1 onion, diced
- 1 and 1/2 tbsp oil

For Water Dough
- 2 cups sifted high protein flour
- a half-cup shortening
- 1 cup water
- 2 tbsp sugar
- 1/4 tsp salt

For Egg Glaze
- 1 lightly beaten egg yolk
- 1 tablespoon evaporated milk

For Seasoning
- 1 tablespoon light soy sauce
- 1 tablespoon oyster sauce
- 3/4 teaspoon thick soy sauce
- 1 tablespoon sugar
- 1/4 teaspoon pepper
- 1/2 teaspoon sesame oil
- 34 cup corn flour

For Oil Dough
- 1 and 1/2 cups sifted high protein flour
- 1 cup shortening

Method:

1. To make the filling, heat 112 tablespoons oil in a nonstick pan and fry the onion until soft, then add the chicken and seasoning and mix well.
2. To combine, toss everything together thoroughly.
3. Remove from the oven and set aside to cool before using.
4. In a mixing bowl, combine the flour, shortening, sugar, salt, and water.
5. To make a smooth dough, combine all of the ingredients.
6. Allow resting for 10 minutes, covered with a damp tea towel.
7. In a mixing bowl, combine the flour and baking powder.
8. Mix in the shortening until a smooth dough forms.
9. Set aside for 10 minutes to rest.
10. Separate the water dough into 40g pieces.
11. Wrap a 25g piece of oil dough in the center.
12. Roll the dough out into a longish flat piece.
13. Roll up like a Swiss roll.
14. Roll it out flat again with a small rolling pin.
15. Then, for the second time, roll up in the Swiss roll fashion.
16. Lay the roll out on a flat surface.
17. Roll out flat and into a circle.
18. 1 heaping tablespoon filling, wrapped
19. Wrap and pleat the fabric to form a pau shape.
20. Place on a round piece of greaseproof paper.
21. Bake for 20–30 minutes, or until lightly golden brown, in a preheated oven at 340 degrees F
22. Remove the buns from the oven and brush with the egg glaze while they are still hot.

BAKE SOY AND SESAME PORK BUNS

Prep Time: 20 minutes
Cooking Time: 60 minutes
Number of Servings: 8

Ingredients:

- 3 cups medium-gluten flour
- 4 cups minced pork
- 1 onion
- 1 cup of water
- 1 teaspoon powdered yeast
- 2 tbsp soy sauce (light)
- 1/2 tbsp. dark soy sauce
- 1 beaten egg, 1/2 teaspoon salt
- 1 tbsp Sesame seeds (optional)

Method:

1. Combine the flour, water, 1 egg, milk, sugar, and yeast in a mixing bowl. Place it in the bread machine and knead it for 10 minutes, or until smooth.
2. Mix in the butter until the dough is well combined. Continue kneading at medium speed for another 10 minutes.
3. Wrapped the dough in a fresh-keeping bag to seal in the fermentation and allow it to double in size. (The fermentation environment is kept at a temperature of around 28°C and a humidity of 70%.)
4. Combine the pork, 1/2 teaspoon salt, pepper, onion, and vegetable oil in a mixing bowl. Set it aside in the refrigerator for storage.
5. Place the dough on a work surface. Add the flour and knead for 10 minutes, or until smooth. Make 12-14 equal-sized pieces of dough.
6. And press small doughs into the wrapper. Scoop 1 tablespoon of pork filling into the center of the dough wrapper. Close the buns.
7. Place the steamed buns on a baking tray and leave them at room temperature for 40 minutes to an hour or until they have doubled in size. (The temperature of the fermentation environment is kept at around 38°C, and the humidity is 85 percent.)
8. Brush the surface of the buns with egg wash and sprinkle with sesame seeds. (optional)
9. Preheat your oven to 180°C/350°F at this time.
10. Bake for 20-25 minutes, or until the buns are golden brown. Serve.

CHINESE HOT DOG FLOWER BUNS

Prep Time: 20 minutes
Cooking Time: 20 minutes
Number of Servings: 8

Ingredients:

For Dough
- 3 cups baking flour
- 1/4 cup sugar 1/2 teaspoon salt 1 teaspoon instant yeast
- Optional: 1 tbsp milk powder
- 1 cup warm whole milk
- Warm 1/3 cup heavy cream
- 1 whole egg

For Assembly
- 8 frankfurters
- 1 yolk of an egg
- 1 tablespoon whole milk
- 1 tablespoon scallions
- 1 tablespoon sesame seeds

Method:

1. Mix bread flour, sugar, salt, instant yeast, and milk powder in a stand mixer fitted with a dough hook. Add the milk, heavy cream, and egg and knead for 10 minutes at low speed. Don't add more flour if the dough is tacky. Cover and leave to rest for 2 hours, or until it has doubled in size.
2. Flour a work surface and divide the dough into 8 equal parts. Tuck and pinch the sides towards the center of each to form a ball. While assembling the flower buns, cover them loosely.
3. Roll out a piece about the width of a hot dog and the length of the hot dog. Put a hot dog in the center, wrap the dough around it and pinch the seam shut. Roll the seam lightly to smooth it out.
4. Cut into 6 pieces and place on a parchment-lined baking sheet. In a flower shape, place one piece in the center and five around it. Repeat with the remaining hot dogs. Allow the buns to rest covered for 30 minutes for a second rise.
5. Preheat the oven to 350 degrees Fahrenheit.
6. Brush the buns with a mixture of egg yolk, and milk. Bake for 20 minutes, then top with scallions and sesame seeds. Serve hot.

STEAMED BUNS

SHANGHAI VEGETARIAN STEAMED BUNS

Prep Time: 20 minutes + 120 Minutes Additional
Cooking Time: 150 minutes
Number of Servings: 10 Steamed Buns

Ingredients:

Steamed Bun Dough
- 1/4 cup lukewarm water
- 1 teaspoon instant yeast
- 2 cups all-purpose white flour
- 1 tablespoon sugar
- 1/4 teaspoon salt

Vegetarian Filling
- 10 large dried shiitake mushrooms 3 tablespoons vegetable oil 5 large bok choy (1 lb)
- ½ tablespoon sesame oil
- 1 teaspoon light soy sauce
- 1/2teaspoon granulated sugar
- 1/4ground white pepper

Method:

1. Soak the dried shiitake mushrooms for 15 minutes in cold water.
2. Heat the vegetable oil in a large skillet over medium heat, then add the mushrooms. Cook for 5 minutes, or until the spices are fragrant.
3. Over high heat, bring a pot of water to a boil. Dip the bok choy for 15 seconds, then drain and rinse under cold water to stop the cooking process. Squeeze the water out of the bok choy with your hands.
4. In a food processor, combine the bok choy and mushrooms. To finely chop the bok choy and mushroom, pulse the mixture a few times. You don't want the mixture to turn into a puree, so don't overmix it. Drain any excess water from the vegetables and place them in a large mixing bowl.
5. Mix in the sesame oil, soy sauce, sugar, and white pepper. Place the bowl in the refrigerator to marinate, covered with plastic wrap.
6. Make the Dough:
7. Whisk together water and yeast in a small bowl until the yeast dissolves.
8. In a large mixing bowl, combine the flour, sugar, and salt. Pour in the yeast mixture and stir with a spatula until the dough forms. Knead the dough with your hands (or a mixer) for about 15 minutes, or until it is smooth and soft. If the dough is too sticky, knead in a teaspoon of flour. If the dough is too dry, a few drops of water can be added.
9. Form the dough into a ball and return it to the bowl. Wrap a chopping board or plastic wrap around the bowl. Allow the dough to rise and double in size at room temperature for 1.5 to 2 hours.
10. Once the dough has risen, knead it for a few minutes to remove any air bubbles. Make 10 even balls out of the dough. 10 pieces of parchment paper, cut into 3x3-inch squares, are set aside.
11. On a lightly floured surface, roll each mini dough ball into a 4-inch circle, adding more flour as needed. It is important to note that the center should be slightly thicker than the edges.
12. Fill the center of each rolled-out dough with 2 tablespoons of filling. Bring

the edges of the dough up, enclose the filling, and pleat the edges together to form a small bag to seal the mixture inside. Each bun should be placed on a single 3x3-inch sheet of parchment paper. Rep until all of the dough and mixture have been used up.

13. Place the buns on a baking sheet and set aside for another 20 minutes to expand.

14. Transfer 5 buns to a steamer pot, cover, and steam over boiling water for 10 minutes. Turn off the heat and set the buns aside for 5 minutes, still covered. DO NOT UNCOVER BEFORE THIS TIME, as doing so will cause the buns to shrink and ruin them. Continue with the remaining 5 buns. Serve right away.

CHINESE STEAMED BUNS WITH BBQ FILLING

Prep Time: 3 Hours
Cooking Time: 15 minutes
Number of Servings: 24Steamed Buns

Ingredients:

- 1 (.25 ounce) envelope active dry yeast
- 1 cup lukewarm water
- 4 1/2 cups all-purpose flour
- 1/4 cup white sugar
- 2 tablespoons shortening or vegetable oil   1/2 cup boiling water
- 2 tablespoons sesame oil
- 2 tablespoons vegetable oil
- 1 green onion, thinly sliced
- 1 clove garlic, minced
- 1/2 pound Asian barbequed pork, cubed
- 2 tablespoons light soy sauce
- 2 tablespoons oyster sauce
- 1 tablespoon white sugar
- 1 tablespoon cornstarch
- 2 tablespoons water

Method:

1. In a large mixing bowl, combine the warm water and the yeast. 1 cup of the flour should be thoroughly mixed in. Cover with a cloth and set aside for 20 minutes, or until bubbles appear.
2. Allow sugar and shortening to dissolve in boiling water and cool to lukewarm. Stir the remaining flour into the yeast mixture. When the dough becomes too stiff to stir, turn it out onto a lightly floured surface and knead for 10 minutes, or until smooth. Coat a large bowl with sesame oil, then add the dough. Cover the bowl with a damp cloth after turning it over to coat. Allow to rise in a warm place until it has doubled in size.
3. In a wok, heat 2 tablespoons oil over medium-high heat. Stir in the green onions and garlic for about 30 seconds. Fry the pork for a minute, then add the soy sauce, oyster sauce, and sugar. Dissolve the cornstarch in 2 tablespoons of water, then stir it into the pork. Cook, stirring constantly, until the pork is coated with a thickened glaze. Transfer to a bowl. Also, allow for cooling.
4. Take the dough out of the bowl and roll it into a long log. Cut the log into 1-inch slices. Use your palm or a rolling pin to flatten each piece into a 3-inch circle. Place 2 tablespoons of the pork filling in the center of each c I circle, gather the edges around the filling, and pinch closed. Place a square of aluminum foil seam side down on top of each bun. Allow to rise for about 1 hour, covered with a towel.
5. In a wok, bring a couple inches of water to a boil. Place a few buns at a time in a steamer, such as a wok steamer or a fitted steam tray. Cover and steam buns for 10 minutes over rapidly boiling water. Rep with the remaining buns.

CHINESE MEATY BUNS

Prep Time: 1 Hour
Cooking Time: 2 Hours
Number of Servings: 24 Steamed Buns

Ingredients:

- 2 and 1/2tablespoons water
- 1 tablespoon white sugar
- Ground black pepper to taste
- 8 ounces chopped pork
- 1 tablespoon rice wine
- 1 tablespoon vegetable oil
- 1 (4 ounces) can think of shrimp
- 1 tablespoon fresh ginger root
- 1 tablespoon light soy sauce
- 2 green onions
- 1 teaspoon salt

Method:

1. In a skillet, cook minced pork over medium-high heat.
2. Set aside to cool after draining and seasoning with salt.
3. Green onions, pepper, sesame oil, white wine, oil, salt, and pepper should be combined.
4. Mix in the minced beef. Add the water and completely mix it in.
5. Preheat the oven to 350°F and prepare the dough for Chinese steamed buns.
6. Form dough balls and tie them around the filling.
7. In a skillet, bring the water to a boil and then reduce the heat to low.
8. Place as many buns on parchment paper as possible.
9. Then use a lid, cover the wok.
10. Heat buns for 20 to 30 minutes over hot water.
11. Steam the buns in groups until they are all finished.

CHINESE STEAMED CHICKEN BUNS

Prep Time: 25 minutes + Rest Time
Cooking Time: 15 minutes
Number of Servings: 24 Steamed Buns

Ingredients:

- 3 dried large shitake mushrooms, 1 pound chicken meat
- 2 tablespoons spring onion, chopped 3 tablespoons cilantro, chopped 2 tablespoons ginger, thinly sliced
- a quarter teaspoon of salt
- a half teaspoon of soy sauce
- 1 tsp sugar 1/4 tsp white pepper
- a quarter teaspoon of sesame oil
- 1 tablespoon rice wine
- 1 tablespoon of water
- cornstarch, 1 tbsp

Method:

1. Soak dried mushrooms in hot water for 2 hours or until soft enough to slice. Remove the stem and throw it away. Cut into matchsticks or a coarse mince.
2. Through the first rise, prepare dough according to our Basic Chinese Dough recipe (x3). Punch dough down, roll into a log, and cut into 24 equal parts on a lightly floured surface. Make a round shape out of each piece of dough. Allow dough to rest in a plastic bag to prevent it from drying out.
3. Cilantro and spring onion should be washed and spun dry. Roughly chop the cilantro. Spring onions should be sliced into rounds. Ginger should be peeled and thinly sliced into 1 1/2 inch long matchsticks.
4. Chicken should be diced into 1/2-inch pieces. Marinate for 15 minutes with cilantro, spring onion, ginger, mushrooms, salt, soy sauce, white pepper, sugar, sesame oil, and rice wine. Combine water and cornstarch in a bowl and stir into the marinated chicken.
5. Kitchen paper should be used to line the steamer. Roll out a round of dough to a 3-inch circle on a lightly floured table. Fill the dough with 1 rounded tbsp of filling. Pleat the circle's edges, pressing firmly until the entire circle is pleated and the filling is wrapped in dough. (Check out our detailed instructions for pleating a bun in our post for Chinese Cha Siu Bao Roasted Pork Buns.)
6. Place 1/2 inch apart in a steamer basket (off heat) and let rise for 10 minutes. Steam for 15 minutes on high heat. Eat hot and delicious, or freeze and reheat to enjoy later. Greetings, Buns!

PERFECT CARROT STEAMED BUNS

Prep Time: 1-2 Hours
Cooking Time: 45 minutes
Number of Servings: 16 Steamed Buns

Ingredients:

Steamed Bun Dough

- 1 cup of hot water
- 2 1/4 teaspoons yeast (active dry)
- 1 teaspoon sugar plus 6 tablespoons
- 2 cups all-purpose flour (plus a little extra for dusting)
- 1 pound of cake flour
- kosher salt (approximately 3/4 teaspoon)
- 2 tbsp. canola oil, plus a little more for the bowl

Filling

- 1 1/4 pound carrots, chopped into 1/2-inch pieces (5 to 7 large)
- 1 tbsp. olive or canola oil
- kosher salt (1/2 teaspoon)
- 6 tbsp. teriyaki sauce plus extra for serving
- 1/4 cup salted roasted peanuts, plus more to serve as a garnish
- 1 tablespoon vinegar (rice)
- 6 scallions, minced, plus more to serve as a garnish
- For drizzling, Sriracha

Method:

1. To make the steamed bun dough, whisk together the water, yeast, and 1 teaspoon of sugar in a small bowl and set aside for 5 minutes, or until foamy on top.
2. Combine the all-purpose flour, cake flour, salt, and the remaining 6 tablespoons of sugar in a large mixing bowl. To make a dough, combine the yeast mixture and the oil in a mixing bowl. Turn out onto a work surface and knead for 5 minutes, or until the dough is smooth and slightly sticky, dusting with flour as needed. Turn the dough into an oiled bowl, cover with plastic wrap or a damp towel, and let it rise for about 2 hours, or until doubled in size.
3. Preheat the oven to 425 degrees Fahrenheit while the dough is rising.
4. In a baking dish, toss the carrots with oil and salt. (I prefer to bake them in a high-sided dish, such as a casserole, so that I have enough room to add the rest of the filling ingredients and don't have to transfer them to a bowl.) Bake for 30 to 35 minutes, or until tender; cool for 5 minutes.
5. Stir together the carrots, teriyaki sauce, peanuts, rice vinegar, scallions, and a drizzle of sriracha. Set aside to cool further. When it's time to fill the buns, it's fine if it's still a little warm. The filling can be prepared and stored in the refrigerator for up to a day.
6. Turn the dough out onto a clean work surface and divide it into 16 balls once it has finished rising. When you're not working with the dough balls, keep them covered. Roll out each ball to a 4 1/2- to 5-inch circle, fill with about 2 heaping tablespoons of filling, and pinch the edges shut to seal well. Place each piece of parchment paper on a 3-inch square. In a steam-

er basket, place the buns 1 1/2 to 2 inches apart. (If your steamer isn't big enough to fit all of the buns at once, steam them in batches.) Cover and allow to rise for another 30 minutes.

7. Over high heat, bring a large pot of water to a boil (the water should come up high in the pot, so it is close to the steamer). Place the steamer over it and steam the buns for 45 minutes, or until light and fluffy.

8. To serve, drizzle with a little more sriracha and sprinkle with peanuts and scallions. Enjoy dipping in teriyaki sauce!

9. Leftovers can be cooled and stored in the refrigerator for up to two days or frozen for three months. Wrap them in a damp paper towel and reheat in the microwave until heated through.

SHANGHAI VEGGIE STEAMED BUNS

Prep Time: 1 Hour
Cooking Time: 20 minutes
Number of Servings: 10 Steamed Buns

Ingredients:

Filling for Vegetarians
- 10 shiitake mushrooms (dried)
- 3 tablespoons oil (vegetable)
- 5 bok choy, large (1 lb)
- 12 tbsp. sesame oil
- 1 teaspoon soy sauce (light)
- 14 ground white pepper 12 teaspoons granulated sugar

Dough for Steamed Buns
- 1/3 cup of lukewarm water
- 1 teaspoon yeast (instant)
- 2 cups white all-purpose flour
- 14 teaspoon salt 12 tablespoon sugar

Method:

How to Make a Vegetarian Filling:
1. Soak the dried shiitake mushrooms for 15 minutes in cold water.
2. Heat the vegetable oil in a large skillet over medium heat before adding the mushrooms. Cook for 5 minutes or until the mixture is fragrant.
3. Over high heat, bring a pot of water to a boil. Dip the bok choy in for 15 seconds, then drain and rinse under cold water to stop the cooking process. Squeeze the water out of the bok choy with your hands.
4. In a food processor, combine the bok choy and mushrooms. Pulse the bok choy and mushroom a few times to finely chop them. You don't want the mixture to turn into a puree, so don't overmix it. Drain any excess water from the vegetables and place them in a large mixing bowl.
5. Mix in the sesame oil, soy sauce, sugar, and white pepper. To marinate, wrap the bowl in plastic wrap and place it in the refrigerator.

Prepare the dough as follows:
6. Whisk together the water and yeast in a small bowl until the yeast is completely dissolved.
7. Combine flour, sugar, and salt in a large mixing bowl. Pour in the yeast mixture and stir until it forms a dough with a spatula. Knead the dough with your hands (or a mixer) for about 15 minutes or until it becomes smooth and soft. Add a teaspoon of flour and knead the dough if it's too sticky. Add a few drops of water if the dough is too dry.
8. Return the dough to the bowl by rolling it into a ball. A chopping board or plastic wrap can be used to cover the bowl. Allow the dough to rise and double in size at room temperature for 1.5 to 2 hours.
9. Knead the dough for a few minutes after it has risen to remove any air bubbles. Make 10 even balls out of the dough.

Assemble and prepare:
10. Cut 10 pieces of parchment paper into 3x3-inch squares and set aside.
11. Roll each mini dough ball into a 4-inch circle on a lightly floured surface, adding

more flour as needed. It's important to keep in mind that the center should be slightly thicker than the edges.

12. Fill the center of each rolled-out dough with 2 tablespoons of filling. Bring the dough's edges up to enclose the filling, then pleat the edges together to form a small bag to seal the mixture inside. Place each bun on a 3x3-inch parchment paper sheet. Rep until you've used up all of the dough and mixture.

13. Place the buns on a baking sheet and set them aside for another 20 minutes to allow them to expand.

14. 5 buns should be placed in a steamer pot, covered, and steamed for 10 minutes over boiling water. Turn off the heat and set the buns aside for 5 minutes, still covered. Do not undercover before this time, as undercover will cause the bun to shrink and ruin them. Carry on with the remaining 5 buns in the same manner. Serve right away.

CHAR SIU BAO

Prep Time: 1 Hour
Cooking Time: 2 Hours
Number of Servings: 8 to 10 Buns

Ingredients:

Dough

- 1 cup warm water (between 100 and 110 degrees Fahrenheit)
- 3 teaspoons of sugar
- 2 1/4 teaspoons dry yeast (1 package)
- 3 14 cups all-purpose flour (approximately 14 2/3 pounds)
- a third of a cup of canola oil
- a quarter teaspoon of salt
- 1 12 tbsp baking powder

Filling

- 12 teaspoon powdered five-spice
- 1 pound trimmed pork tenderloin
- 1 cup green onions, thinly sliced
- a third of a cup of hoisin sauce
- 2 tbsp rice wine vinegar
- 1 tablespoon soy sauce (low sodium)
- 1 and a half teaspoons honey
- 1 teaspoon fresh ginger, peeled and minced
- 1 teaspoon garlic, minced
- a quarter teaspoon of salt

Method:

1. To make the filling, evenly coat the pork with five-spice powder. Preheat a grill pan to medium-high. Spray the pan with nonstick cooking spray. Cook, turning pork occasionally, for 18 minutes or until a thermometer registers 155°. Remove the pork from the pan and set it aside for 15 minutes.
2. Pork should be cut crosswise into thin slices, and the slices should be cut into thin strips. Put the pork in a medium mixing bowl. Stir in the onions and the remaining 7 ingredients (through 1/4 teaspoon salt) until everything is well combined. Cover and store in the refrigerator.
3. In a large mixing bowl, combine 1 cup warm water, sugar, and yeast; set aside for 5 minutes.
4. Fill dry measuring cups halfway with flour and level with a knife. Toss the yeast mixture with the flour, oil, and 1/4 teaspoon salt, and stir until a soft dough forms. Turn out the dough onto a floured surface. Knead until the dough is smooth and elastic (about 10 minutes). Place dough in a large mixing bowl that has been sprayed with cooking spray and turn to coat the top. Cover and set aside for 1 hour or until doubled in size in a warm (85°) draft-free environment. (Press two fingers gently into the dough.) If the indentation remains, the dough has risen sufficiently.)
5. Allow dough to rest for 5 minutes after punching it down. Place the dough on a clean surface and knead in the baking powder. Allow dough to rest for 5 minutes.
6. Make 10 equal portions of dough and roll each one into a ball. Roll one dough ball at a time into a 5-inch circle (cover remaining dough balls to keep them from drying out). 1/4 cup filling in the center of the dough circle Brings up the sides to cover the filling and bring them together on top. Pinch the edges together and twist to close. Continue with the remaining dough balls and filling.
7. In each tier of a 2-tiered bamboo steamer, arrange 5 buns seam side down, 1 inch apart. Stack the tiers and cover them with the lid.
8. Fill a large skillet halfway with water and bring to a boil over medium-high heat. Steam for 15 minutes, or until puffed and set, in a steamer. Allow 10 minutes for cooling before serving.

TENDER SOFT MANTOU

Prep Time: 10 minutes
Cooking Time: 20 minutes
Number of Servings: 8 BUns

Ingredients:

- 1 cup of milk
- 1 teaspoon dried active yeast
- sugar, 2 1/2 tablespoons
- 2 3/4 cup flour (all-purpose)

Method:

1. In the bowl of a stand mixer fitted with a dough hook, combine the milk, yeast, and sugar. Using chopsticks or a spoon, stir the mixture.
2. Combine the flour and yeast in a mixing bowl. Turn the mixer to speed 1 and knead the ingredients for about 6 minutes, or until a smooth dough forms. Stop the stand mixer and push the dough down to the bowl if it starts to "climb up" the dough hook.
3. Cover the dough with plastic wrap and set aside for 5 minutes to rest.
4. Roll out the dough with a rolling pin from bottom to top on a lightly floured surface.
5. Roll the dough horizontally from the bottom to the top.
6. Continue rolling out the dough to make a 14x10-inch rectangle. "The shape is rectangular.
7. From left to right, roll the dough into a log. Make sure the dough is tucked and rolled into a tight log.
8. Roll the log out a few times or until the surface is smooth and the length is 12 inches.
9. Using a sharp knife, cut the dough into 8 equal-sized pieces. Place each dough ball in a 3x4 baking pan "a sheet of parchment paper with a thickness of -inch. After cutting the dough, roll it into a round ball.
10. In a steamer, place the dough. Allow the dough balls to rise in the steamer for 60 minutes or until they have doubled in size. Make sure each dough ball has enough space between them, so they don't stick together.
11. Fill the bottom of the steamer with water. To make the steamed buns whiter, add 1 teaspoon Chinese white vinegar. Tightly close the lid.
12. Steam for 10-12 minutes, or until the dough expands to soft, puffy, and fluffy steamed buns on high heat. Remove the steamed buns from the heat and serve them warm. If you like sweet steamed buns, try dipping them in condensed milk.

CRANBERRY AND PUMPKIN STEAM BUNS

Prep Time: 20 minutes
Cooking Time: 20 minutes
Number of Servings: 9 Small Steamed Buns

Ingredients:

- active dry yeast (1 teaspoon)
- granulated sugar (2 tablespoons)
- water (1/2 cup)
- vegetable oil (2 tablespoons)
- pumpkin puree (1/2 cup)
- all-purpose flour (2 + 1/2 cups)
- teaspoon ground cinnamon
- salt (V2 teaspoon)
- 1 cup dried cranberries

Method:

1. Dissolve yeast and sugar in water in a medium mixing bowl. Incorporate the oil and pumpkin puree until smooth and uniform. Allow for a few minutes.
2. In a large mixing bowl, combine the flour, cinnamon, and salt. Pour in the yeast mixture and combine thoroughly, scraping down the sides of the bowl as needed (there should be no dry flour particles visible).
3. Knead the dough for 5 minutes on a clean surface, or until it forms a smooth dough ball.
4. Return the dough to the mixing bowl and coat with a little oil to keep it from drying out. Cover the bowl with plastic wrap and set it aside at room temperature for 1 hour to double in size.
5. Transfer the dough to a lightly oiled clean surface and punch the air out of the dough ball. Using a rolling pin, flatten and shape the dough into an approximately 9x16-inch rectangle.
6. Distribute the dried cranberries evenly on top of the dough. Roll the dough carefully into a log and cut it into 8 equal pieces with a knife or bench scraper.
7. Line a steamer basket with parchment paper and lightly oil it (to prevent the buns from sticking during steaming). Arrange the buns in an even layer on top. Fill a large pot halfway with water, about 1 or 2 inches deep. At no time should the water level rise above the steamer basket. Cover the pot with the lid and place the steamer basket on top. Allow the buns to rise for 15–20 minutes. You don't have to wait for the buns to double in size because they will rise during the steaming process.
8. Bring the water to a boil in a large pot over high heat. After that, reduce the heat to medium-high and steam the buns for 15 minutes over boiling water. Turn off the heat and leave the buns in the steamer for 5 more minutes before removing them. This will keep the buns from shrinking as the temperature drops.
9. Serve and have fun!

BAOZI

Prep Time: 25 minutes
Cooking Time: 3 hours
Number of Servings: 12 Steamed Buns

Ingredients:

Making The Dough
- 6 tbsp. Water 2 tbsp. cornstarch
- 1 tbsp. honey or sweetened condensed milk
- 1 tsp. instant yeast 3/4 cup milk, divided
- 3 1/3 cup flour (all-purpose)
- kosher salt (approximately 3/4 teaspoon)

Pork Filling
- 1 1/4 cup cabbage, finely shredded
- kosher salt, 1 tsp
- 1 pound minced or ground pork
- a quarter teaspoon of five-spice
- 1/2 teaspoon Szechuan peppercorns, ground
- 1/4 teaspoon coriander powder
- 1 tsp. white pepper, ground
- 1 tsp. black pepper, freshly ground
- MSG (1/2 teaspoon) (optional)
- a half "finely minced ginger
- 2 garlic cloves, finely minced
- 1/4 cup chives or green onions, finely chopped
- 2 tsp soy sauce (low sodium)
- 1 teaspoon sesame oil, toasted

Miso Carrot Filling
- 8 oz. firm tofu or fish cakes, finely diced 2 large carrots, shredded
- a "2 green onions, thinly sliced 1 piece fresh ginger, grated 1 large garlic clove, grated
- 3 tablespoons miso
- 1 tsp. black pepper, freshly ground
- 1/2 tsp. Ground cayenne or 1 tbsp. gochugaru
- 1 tbsp. sesame oil, toasted
- 1 tablespoon sesame seeds, toasted

Red Bean Paste Filling
- 1 cup dried adzuki beans, soaked in water overnight
- kosher salt (1/2 teaspoon)
- 2/3 cup sugar, granulated
- Dipping Sauce
- a quarter cup of Chinese black vinegar
- 4 tsp sesame oil, toasted
- 1 teaspoon fresh ginger, finely minced (optional)
- granulated sugar, 1/2 teaspoon
- 1 tsp. kosher salt

Method:

1. Whisk together cornstarch and water in a small pot over low heat. Cook for 1 to 2 minutes, or until the sauce has thickened. Remove from the heat and whisk in the honey and 14 cups milk until smooth. Allow the mixture to cool to lukewarm before whisking in the yeast.
2. Heat the remaining 12 cups of milk until it begins to simmer. Combine flour, salt, and hot milk in a large mixing bowl with chopsticks or a fork until a shaggy mixture forms. Stir in the cornstarch-yeast mixture and knead the dough with your hands for about 5 minutes, or until it is cohesive and no dry spots remain. Allow dough to rest for 30 minutes in a covered bowl.
3. Gently deflate the dough, then pick up one edge and gently pull it toward the opposite edge to fold it. Repeat the stretch and fold motion around the bowl for a to-

tal of four folds, then flip the dough over, so the smooth side is facing up. Allow for another 30 minutes of resting time. Repeat the stretch and fold process two more times, pausing for about 30 minutes between folds.

4. In the meantime, prepare your filling of choice. Make the savory dipping sauce if desired: In a small mixing bowl, whisk together all the sauce ingredients until smooth.

5. Cut dough into 12 equal pieces when ready to assemble buns. Working with one piece of dough at a time, roll each into a 6" round on a lightly floured surface, rotating the dough frequently and making sure the edges are thinner than the center.

6. In the center of the round, place a portioned meatball or 2 tablespoons of filling, then pleat the edges together. Gather and pinch together 34" of dough, repeating this motion all around the edge of the round, between 12 and 15 pleats total, using your dominant hand's thumb, middle, and index finger to hold all the pleats in one spot while the other hand "feeds" the dough into the fold: Gently twist your pleats counterclockwise to create a swirl pattern, then pinch to firmly seal them together.

7. Fill a large pot halfway with cold water and place a steamer basket on top. Cut twelve 3" squares of parchment, then place buns 2" apart on prepared parchment inside the steamer. Allow rising for 30 minutes to 1 hour, uncovered, until the dough has doubled in size and springs back slowly when poked.

8. Turn the heat to medium and cover the pot with a lid lined with a paper towel (to trap condensation). Reduce heat to low and steam buns for 10 minutes once the water has reached a boil. Turn off the heat and leave the lid on for another 5 minutes. Remove the lid and set aside until the buns are cool enough to handle.

9. If desired, serve with a dipping sauce.

10. Toss cabbage with salt in a large mixing bowl until well combined. Allow for a 10-minute rest period.

11. Stir in the rest of the pork filling ingredients in one direction until smooth paste forms.

12. Portion the mixture into 12 meatballs on a plate or tray lined with parchment paper and freeze for 30 minutes or until semi-firm.

13. Combine all ingredients in a large mixing bowl and stir until well combined.

14. While the dough is resting, place it in the refrigerator to chill.

15. Soaked beans should be rinsed and drained. Bring the beans, 2 cups water, and salt to a boil in a medium pot over medium heat. Reduce heat to a low simmer and cook for 30 minutes, or until beans are tender and split. Drain the cooking liquid and set it aside.

16. Return the pot with the beans to a medium-low heat setting. Add the sugar and just enough cooking liquid to barely cover the beans (about 12 to 23 cups) and cook for 15 minutes, or until the beans are completely creamy and the liquid has been absorbed. Mash the beans with a wooden spoon or a potato masher until they reach the desired consistency.

17. Before using, allow cooling completely.

CHINESE BREAD

HEARTY ALMOND BREAD

Prep Time: 10-20 minutes
Cooking Time: 60 minutes
Number of Servings: 8

Ingredients:

- 3 cups almond flour
- 1 teaspoon baking soda
- 2 teaspoons baking powder
- ¼ teaspoon salt
- ¼ cup almond milk
- ½ cup + 2 tablespoons olive oil
- 3 whole eggs

Method:

1. Pre-heat your oven to 300 degrees F
2. Grease a 9x5 inch loaf pan and keep it on the side
3. Add the listed ingredients and mix them, transfer batter to prepared loaf pan
4. Bake for 60 minutes
5. Once baked, remove from oven and let it cool
6. Slice and enjoy!

PERFECT CINNAMON BREAD

Prep Time: 10-20 minutes
Cooking Time: 25-30 minutes
Number of Servings: 8

Ingredients:

- 3 pastured eggs
- 1 teaspoon vinegar
- 3 tablespoons salted butter
- 2 tablespoons water
- ½ cup coconut flour
- ½ teaspoon baking soda
- 1 teaspoon cinnamon
- ½ teaspoon baking powder
- 1/3 cup pure sour cream
- 1/8 teaspoon stevia

Method:

1. Pre-heat your oven to 350 degrees F
2. Take a loaf pan and oil it, line the bottom with parchment paper
3. Mix dry ingredients in a bowl and whisk well
4. Add remaining ingredients to the dry mix and mix well, taste for sweetness
5. Adjust seasoning
6. Let the mix stand for 3 minutes
7. Spread batter onto loaf pan and bake for 25-30 minutes
8. Cool loaf and enjoy!

EGG AND COCONUT BREAD

Prep Time: 10-20 minutes
Cooking Time: 40 minutes
Number of Servings: 8

Ingredients:

- 4 whole eggs
- 1 cup water
- 2 tablespoons apple cider vinegar
- ¼ cup + 1 teaspoon coconut oil, melted
- ½ teaspoon garlic powder
- ½ cup coconut flour
- ½ teaspoon baking soda
- ¼ teaspoon Coarse salt

Method:

1. Pre-heat your oven to 350 degrees F
2. Grease a baking tin with 1 teaspoon coconut oil, keep it on the side
3. Add eggs to blender alongside water, vinegar, ¼ cup coconut oil, blend for half a minute
4. Add garlic powder, baking soda, coconut flour, salt and blend for a minute
5. Transfer to the baking tin
6. Bake for 40 minutes
7. Serve and enjoy!

LOVELY CHINESE FLATBREAD

Prep Time: 10-20 minutes
Cooking Time: 10 minutes
Number of Servings: 8

Ingredients:

- 1 and ½ tablespoons coconut flour
- ¼ teaspoon baking powder
- 1/8 teaspoon salt
- 1 tablespoon coconut oil, melted
- 1 whole egg

Method:

1. Pre-heat your oven to 350 degrees F
2. Add coconut flour, baking powder, salt
3. Add coconut oil, eggs and stir well until mixed
4. Leave the batter for several minutes
5. Pour half batter onto a baking pan
6. Spread it to form a circle, repeat with the remaining batter
7. Bake in the oven for 10 minutes
8. Once a golden brown texture comes, let it cool and serve
9. Enjoy!

LOVELY EGG MUFFIN

Prep Time: 10-20 minutes
Cooking Time: 25 minutes
Number of Servings: 6

Ingredients:

- 1 tablespoon olive oil
- 1 cup green pepper, chopped
- 1 cup red pepper, chopped
- 1 cup yellow onion, chopped
- 1 cup mushrooms, chopped
- 2 cups baby spinach, chopped
- 2 garlic cloves, minced
- Salt to taste
- 4 egg whites
- 4 whole eggs

Method:

1. Pre-heat your oven to 350 degrees F
2. Grease muffin tins and keep them on the side
3. Pre-heat a large skillet on medium-high heat and pour oil, add peppers and onion, Saute for 5 minutes
4. Once the veggies are tender, add mushrooms, spinach and Saute for 2 minutes
5. Add garlic and cook for ½ minute
6. Season with salt and pepper, remove heat
7. Whisk in eggs and add Sautéed veggies in a bowl
8. Pour egg mixture into muffin tins and bake for 20 minutes
9. Serve and enjoy!

AWESOME ASIAN MILK BREAD

Prep Time: 10-20 minutes
Cooking Time: 25 minutes
Number of Servings: 8

Ingredients:

- 9 oz. bread flour/all-purpose flour
- 1 teaspoon instant yeast 2.5 tablespoons sugar 1/3 teaspoon salt
- 1 large, room-temperature egg
- 1/2 gallon of hot milk
- 2 tbsp unsalted butter (at room temperature)
- 1 egg was whisked together with 1 teaspoon of water to make an egg wash.

Method:

1. In a large mixing bowl, combine all-purpose flour, sugar, salt, and instant yeast.
2. Make a well in the center, pour in the egg and warm milk, stir to form a shaggy mass, and knead until smooth.
3. Knead in the unsalted butter for 15-20 minutes, or until the dough is smooth and elastic.
4. Butter an 8"x3" round baking pan. Divide the dough into eight equal parts, roll each into a ball, and place in the pan. (1) (Note 1)
5. Cover the pan with a wet kitchen towel and proof in a warm kitchen for one hour or until the dough fills the pan.
6. Preheat the oven to 175 degrees Fahrenheit (350 Fahrenheit). Brush the egg wash over the top of the dough and bake for 20-25 minutes, or until golden brown.
7. Remove the bread from the oven and cool for 10 minutes in the pan before gently removing it and cooling completely on a wire rack.
8. Any leftovers should be kept in an airtight container. At room temperature, it will keep for up to 3 days. If you prefer warm bread, reheat for 10 seconds in the microwave before serving.

CHINESE BREAD PACKETS

Prep Time: 10-20 minutes
Cooking Time: 10-15 minutes
Number of Servings: 8

Ingredients:

- 4 slices of bread
- Oil as needed
- 3 - Medium boiled and mashed potatoes
- 1 Onion
- 2 - Finely chopped green chilies
- 1/2 teaspoon ginger, grated
- ½ capsicum
- 2 spring onions
- Coriander
- Salt as needed
- 2 teaspoons soy sauce
- 2 teaspoons chili sauce
- 1 tablespoon vinegar

Method:

1. In a shallow pan, heat 1 tablespoon of oil and add all the stuffing in-gredients, except the potatoes and sauces.
2. Toss in the potatoes now.
3. After that, add in the soy sauce, chili sauce, and vinegar.
4. 1 slice of bread should be dipped in water for a few seconds before gently pressing.
5. Place one portion of the stuffing in the center of the bread vertically.
6. Bring both sides of the bread, slice together, and squeeze out all the water between your hands.
7. Set aside for now.
8. Make a total of three more packets.
9. Fry until golden brown in a deep fryer.
10. Serve with a side of tomato sauce.

THE PERFECT SCALLION BING

Prep Time: 10-20 minutes + Rest Time
Cooking Time: 20 minutes
Number of Servings: 8

Ingredients:

Mixture of Yeast
- 14 cup hot water
- 1 tsp yeast 2 tsp sugar
- sesame oil, 2 tbsp

Coating
- Brush with sesame or neutral oil.
- 1/4 cup sesame seeds to 1/2 cup sesame seeds

For Prep
- Oil with a neutral pH

Dough
- 2 cups all-purpose flour (255g) plus additional flour to flour your work surface
- 1 teaspoon salt Filling and Mixing
- a quarter teaspoon of white pepper
- a quarter teaspoon of salt, or more to taste (see notes)
- a quarter teaspoon of five-spice powder
- 3/4 cup scallions, finely chopped
- Brush with sesame or neutral oil.
- sesame seeds, 1 tbsp

Method:

1. To learn how to make these from scratch, watch the video below or follow the steps above.
2. Combine the warm water, sugar, and yeast in a measuring cup or bowl. Set aside after thoroughly mixing.
3. Allow 5 minutes for the yeast to foam up in the mixture. Mix in the oil after it has foamed up.
4. In a large mixing bowl, combine the flour and salt. Mix thoroughly.
5. In the center of the bowl, make a well and pour in the yeast mixture. Mix everything together with a pair of chopsticks or a spatula to make a dough.
6. This can also be done with a stand mixer. I simply kneaded everything together with my hands.
7. Knead for 5-6 minutes, or until you have a dough ball that does not stick to your hands. Scrape the sides of the bowl to remove any excess flour.
8. In the bowl, place the dough ball.
9. Using a damp towel, cover the bowl. Allow the dough to rise for at least 1 hour in a warm place until it has doubled in size.
10. If you want to make the dough ahead of time and store it in the refrigerator, follow the steps under 'Making the Dough in Advance' below.
11. Combine the white pepper, 5 spice powder, and salt in a small bowl to make the spice mix.
12. Set aside the scallions in a bowl after finely chopping them.
13. Flour your work surface lightly.
14. Place the dough ball on the surface.
15. Flour your rolling pin lightly. After that, roll out the dough ball.
16. Continue rolling until you have a large rectangular sheet of dough that measures 14 by 9 inches (36 x 22 cm). Don't be concerned if it isn't a perfect rectangle. The dough should be about a third of an inch thick (less than 1 cm).

17. Brush a thin layer of oil on the dough's surface once it has been rolled out.
18. Sprinkle all of the spice mixtures evenly over the dough piece.
19. After that, distribute the scallions evenly across the dough.
20. Finally, toss in the sesame seeds.
21. Roll the bing from one end once all of the toppings are in place.
22. You'll end up with a log that's similar to a cinnamon roll.
23. To completely seal the edges, pinch them together.
24. Using a knife, cut the long roll in half.
25. After that, roll one piece of the dough inwards to form a spiral (like a snail). Underneath the ends, tuck them in.
26. Rep with the second piece of dough. To keep the bing from drying out, cover it with plastic wrap.
27. Brush a thin layer of oil onto a large chopping board or a flat surface.
28. Place a rolled bing piece on the surface. If necessary, lightly flour your rolling pin.
29. Roll out the bing into an 8" circle by pressing down on the dough.
30. Brush a thin layer of sesame seeds on the exposed side, and then sprinkle 1-2 tbsp sesame seeds on top.
31. To help the sesame seeds stick to the dough, lightly press them down.
32. Flip the rolled-out bing carefully over. You can use a large spatula or your hands to do this. Add a couple of tablespoons of sesame seeds and pat them down as well.
33. Transfer the bing to a plate or leave it on the board. Before cooking, cover it with a towel and set it aside for 15 minutes to rest.
34. Roll out the remaining rolled bing in the same manner until you have two 8-inch bings.
35. Over medium-high heat, heat a large nonstick or cast iron pan. Follow the steps below to cook this dish without using any additional oil.
36. Using some oil, coat the pan's surface. Place the bing on the pan once the oil is hot. Cook for 4-5 minutes over medium-high heat, or until golden brown and crisp.
37. Cover your pan after carefully flipping the bing. Because the bing is quite thick, this will aid in the cooking of the insides. Allow another 4-5 minutes for the pancake to cook and crisp up on the other side.
38. Because of the yeast, the bing will fluff up and rise a little higher.
39. Remove the cover and inspect the other side. If it's golden brown and crisp on one side, you can flip it and crisp the other side even more. Both sides should have a golden brown color to them.
40. Tap the bing gently with your finger or spatula. On the outside, it should sound crisp and hollow.
41. Transfer the bing to a plate or chopping board after removing it from the pan. Allow cooling for a couple of minutes before slicing.
42. Cook the remaining bing in the same manner until both pieces are done.
43. I simply sliced each piece into four pieces for the bing. As a result, I ended up with a total of eight pieces.
44. Enjoy your bing while they're still hot, so the outside is crispy, and the inside is fluffy and aromatic.

ROAST PORK GARLIC BREAD

Prep Time: 10-20 minutes
Cooking Time: 20 minutes
Number of Servings: 4

Ingredients:

- 1 1/4 pound pork tenderloin, cut in half crosswise
- seasoning with salt and pepper
- 1/4 cup of hoisin sauce
- 3 tablespoons of honey
- 8 garlic cloves, finely chopped and ground into a paste
- 2 tbsp sesame seed oil
- 1 pound (4 ounces) room temperature butter
- 1 large loaf of Italian bread, split lengthwise in half
- 14 cup duck sauce from the store

Method:

1. Preheat the oven to 450 degrees and place the rack in the lower third. Preheat the oven to 350°F and season the pork with salt and pepper.
2. Combine 3 tablespoons of hoisin sauce, honey, 1 teaspoon garlic, and sesame oil in a small bowl; set aside half.
3. Brush the other half of the hoisin mixture over the pork in a small roasting pan. Roast for about 20 minutes, or until an instant-read thermometer reads 150 degrees. Place on a cutting board to cool.
4. Meanwhile, combine the butter and remaining garlic in a mixing bowl. Spread the garlic butter on the bread halves, wrap them in foil, and bake for 10 minutes.
5. Open the foil and bake the bread cut side up for 5 minutes, or until toasted.
6. Combine the reserved hoisin mixture and the remaining 1 table-spoon hoisin sauce in a bowl. Pork should be thinly sliced. Toss the vegetables in the bowl to coat them.
7. Place the pork on the bottom of the bread and drizzle with the duck sauce.
8. Place the top of the bread on top and cut crosswise into quarters.
9. Serve and Enjoy!

PERFECTLY FRIED CHINESE BREAD

Prep Time: 255 minutes
Cooking Time: 30 minutes
Number of Servings: 8

Ingredients:

- 1/3 teaspoon sugar
- 1/3 teaspoon salt
- 11 tablespoons water
- 1 and 2/3 tablespoons yeast
- 1 and 2/3 cups flour

Method:

1. Using a pinch of sugar, dissolve the yeast in lukewarm water. Allow it to rise before adding it to the sifted flour, adding salt, and beginning to mix. Knead for about 8 minutes, or until the dough is smooth and elastic.
2. Allow it to rise in a warm place for 2 hours or until it has doubled in size.
3. Then knead it for a few minutes more and let it rise for another 2 hours. After that, roll it out to a length of 23.5″ (60 cm) and a diameter of 2″. (5 cm). It should be cut into 2″ thick pieces (5 cm).
4. Roll out each piece, lightly brush with oil, and shape it into florets or other curled shapes.
5. After steaming the buns for 20 minutes, fry them in hot oil until golden. Serve with sesame seeds and soy sauce, if desired.

UNIQUE COOKIES

CHINESE ALMOND COOKIE

Prep Time: 10-20 minutes + Dough Chill Time 2 Hours
Cooking Time: 15 minutes
Number of Servings: 60

Ingredients:

- 1 and 1/3 cups almond flour, packed
- Thinly sliced almonds
- ½ teaspoon baking soda
- 1 cup + 2 tablespoons sugar
- 1 and ¾ cups all-purpose flour
- 1 teaspoon almond extract
- 2 large eggs, divide
- Pinch of salt
- 1 cup butter, unsalted, cut into cubes

Method:

1. In a stand mixer fitted with a paddle attachment, beat the almond flour, salt, and butter for 3 minutes on medium speed. The mixture will become coarse and chunky in appearance.
2. Combine one of the eggs and the almond extract
3. At low speed, mix them in until just combined.
4. Sift in the flour, sugar, and baking soda: Sift in the flour, sugar, and baking soda.
5. At low speed, mix until just combined.
6. Chill the dough by flattening it into a disc and wrapping it in plastic wrap. Chill it in the refrigerator for two hours.
7. Preheat the oven to 325 degrees Fahrenheit. Preheat the oven to 350°F. Line a baking sheet with parchment paper.
8. Beat the remaining egg in a small bowl.
9. Roll out pieces of dough into 3/4-inch-wide balls. Place them about an inch apart on the sheet, then press them down slightly with your palm to form a coin shape.
10. Each cookie should have one silvered almond in the center. Then, using a pastry brush or your finger, paint the egg onto each cookie. (When the cookie bakes, it will have a lacquered appearance.)
11. Bake at 325°F for 13 to 15 minutes, or until the edges begin to tan. Cool on a wire rack on a sheet of parchment paper.

THE PERFECT FORTUNE COOKIE

Prep Time: 10 minutes
Cooking Time: 10 minutes
Number of Servings: 15

Ingredients:

- 2 egg whites
- 1 tablespoon vanilla extract
- 1 tablespoon almond extract
- 3 tablespoons sunflower oil
- 100g unbleached flour
- 100g caster sugar 2 tsp cornflour
- 12 tablespoons black sesame seeds

Method:

1. Preheat the oven to 360°F and line a large baking sheet with parchment paper or a silicone baking sheet. Fortunes should be written or printed on 6cm long by 1cm wide paper.
2. In a mixing bowl, whisk together the egg whites, vanilla, almond extract, oil, and 2 tablespoons cold water with an electric hand whisk until frothy, 20-30 seconds. Sift the flour, cornflour, sugar, and a generous pinch of salt into the egg white mixture.
3. Whisk everything together until it resembles a smooth batter. Refrigerate the mixture for 1 hour.
4. Place a tbsp of the mixture on the prepared baking sheet. Using the back of a metal spoon, swirl the mixture out into an 8-10cm circle. Repeat with a second tablespoon of the mixture to make two cookies.
5. Allow enough space between each cookie because they will spread in the oven. It's best to only bake 2-3 cookies at a time because you'll need to shape them while they're still hot. 1 of the cookies should be sprinkled with black sesame seeds before baking for 10-12 minutes or until the edges of the cookies turn golden.
6. Once the cookies have cooled, remove them from the oven one at a time with a palette knife. You want them to be soft so that you can shape them quickly. Turn the cookie over so that the sesame seeds face down and center the fortune in the circle.
7. To secure the fortune, fold the circle in half and pinch the two edges together to seal. Place the cookie on the rim of a mug or cup and gently pull the two corners down to form a fortune cookie.
8. Hold for 10 seconds before transferring the cookies to muffin tins to keep their shape while cooling completely.
9. Repeat with the rest of the cookie dough.

CHINESE BUTTER COOKIE

Prep Time: 10-20 minutes
Cooking Time: 15 minutes
Number of Servings: 40 Small Cookies

Ingredients:

- 12 tbsp (1 1/2 sticks) softened unsalted butter
- 3/4 cup granulated sugar
- 1 single large egg
- 1/2 teaspoon of pure vanilla extract
- 1 and 1/2 cup self-rising flour

Method:

1. Preheat the oven to 375 degrees Fahrenheit. Preheat the oven to 350°F. Line a baking sheet with parchment paper.
2. Cream the butter in a standing electric mixer until smooth. Cream in the confectioners' sugar until fluffy. Combine the egg and vanilla extract in a mixing bowl. Sift in the self-rising flour gradually and beat until a smooth dough forms.
3. Attach a star or flower-shaped disk to the dough in a cookie press. Place the cookies on a baking sheet lined with parchment paper, leaving 1 inch of space around each cookie.
4. Bake for 15 minutes, or until the top is lightly golden. Allow cooling completely on a wire rack before storing. The cookies can be stored in an airtight container at room temperature for 3 to 4 days.

DELIGHTFUL CHINESE SESAME COOKIES

Prep Time: 10-20 minutes + Chill Time
Cooking Time: 20 minutes
Number of Servings: 24-25

Ingredients:

- 2 cups of All-Purpose flour
- 1 tablespoon of baking powder
- 1/2 teaspoon of baking soda
- 1/2 cup butter
- ¼ teaspoon of salt
- ½ cup of shortening
- 3/4 cup granulated sugar
- a quarter cup brown sugar
- 1 whole egg
- 1 teaspoon of almond essence
- 1/3 cup of white sesame seeds

Method:

1. Collect all of the ingredients.
2. In a medium mixing bowl, combine the flour, baking powder, baking soda, and salt.
3. In a large mixing bowl, cream the butter, shortening, white and brown sugars, and vanilla extract.
4. Beat in the eggs and almond extract until well combined.
5. Mix in the flour mixture thoroughly. At this point, the dough will be dry and crumbly.
6. Form the mixture into a dough with your fingers, then shape it into two 10 to 12 inch long rolls or logs. Wrap in plastic wrap and place in the refrigerator for at least 2 hours, preferably 4 hours. (If desired, make the dough ahead of time and refrigerate it overnight.)
7. Preheat the oven to 325 degrees Fahrenheit.
8. Take a log and lightly score it at 3/4 inch intervals to make 15 pieces, then cut the dough.
9. Roll each piece into a small ball and roll it in the sesame seed bowl to coat. (Note: If desired, brush the ball with a lightly beaten egg before dipping it in the sesame seeds to help the seeds adhere to the cookie.)
10. Place the balls 2 inches apart on a lightly greased cookie sheet.
11. Bake the cookies for 15 to 17 minutes, or until a fork inserted into the center comes out clean, and they easily lift from the baking sheet. Allow cooling completely.
12. When completely cool, serve or store in a tightly sealed container.

TASTY MAZOLA PEANUT COOKIES

Prep Time: 10-20 minutes + Dough Chill Time 2 Hours
Cooking Time: 15 minutes
Number of Servings: 60

Ingredients:

- 4 tablespoons peanut butter
- 5.3 tablespoons icing sugar
- 1.4 cup plain flour
- 1 teaspoon baking powder
- 12 teaspoon salt
- 3.3 tbsp cooking oil (you can use any neutral-tasting oil, such as mazola oil) Begin with this amount gradually.
- 1 egg yolk + 1 tablespoon water

Method:

1. Preheat the oven to 350 degrees Fahrenheit. To make the egg wash, lightly beat the egg yolk with 1 teaspoon of water. Set aside some time
2. If you're using natural peanut butter or another nut butter, give it a good stir before adding it to the recipe.
3. Combine the ground peanuts or peanut butter, sugar, flour, baking powder, and salt in a large mixing bowl. With a wooden spoon, stir to combine. Then slowly drizzle in the cooking oil (don't pour it all in at once); you may not need all of it. Stir until the dough comes together and can be pressed together to form a dough. If it's too dry, add a little more oil until the dough doesn't fall apart. The peanut butter dough is a little sticky, but you can dust your fingers with flour to help you roll it into balls.
4. Form the dough into balls (how big or small you want them to be is entirely up to you). Each of mine weighs about 10 g. Place them about 1/2 inch apart on a cookie sheet lined with parchment paper; they don't expand much. Carry on with the rest.
5. I created three distinct styles. Make a small indentation in the center with a straw (mine are a bit too deep). You can also use a fork to gently press the dough ball down while making the crisscross pattern or simply place a half-peanut on top of the cookie dough.
6. Brush the egg wash over the cookies and bake for about 15 minutes, or until golden brown. Add another 5 minutes if you want a crisper texture. Remove from the oven and cool for about 10 minutes before transferring to a cooling rack to cool completely. When they are warm, they become extremely soft. Store at room temperature in an airtight container for up to 1 month.

GINGER ALMOND COOKIES

Prep Time: 10-20 minutes
Cooking Time: 10 minutes
Number of Servings: 42 Cookies

Ingredients:

- 1 pound of shortening
- 12 cup sugar + (4 tbsp) additional for rolling
- 14 cup brown sugar, packed
- a single large egg
- 2 cups all-purpose flour 1 teaspoon almond extract
- 12 tablespoons baking powder
- 14 teaspoon salt
- 1/3 cup finely chopped candied ginger
- Almonds, sliced

Method:

1. Preheat the oven to 350 degrees Fahrenheit.
2. Cream shortening, 12 cup sugar, and brown sugar together in a stand mixer bowl or a large mixing bowl with a hand mixer until light and fluffy.
3. Combine the egg and almond extract in a mixing bowl. Mix everything together thoroughly.
4. Whisk together the flour, baking soda, and salt in a medium mixing bowl, then gradually add to the sugar mixture.
5. Add the ginger and mix well.
6. Form small 1-inch balls with a teaspoon. In the remaining sugar, roll them.
7. Place 2 inches apart on parchment-lined baking sheets or ungreased baking sheets. Flatten the cookies with the bottom of a sugar-dusted glass or measuring cup. In the center of each cookie, place a sliced almond.
8. Bake for 9-11 minutes, or until light brown around the edges. Allow cooling for a few minutes on the sheets. Allow cooling completely on wire racks. Keep the container airtight.

BUTTERY CHINESE WALNUT COOKIES

Prep Time: 10-20 minutes
Cooking Time: 60 minutes
Number of Servings: 20 Cookies

Ingredients:

To make the topping

- 1/2 cup minuscule (50 grams) halves and pieces of walnut
- 1/4 cup (55 grams) light brown sugar, packed
- 1/4 cup (20 grams) desiccated coconut, unsweetened
- 3 tablespoons melted unsalted butter
- 1 1/2 teaspoons powdered five-spice

To make the cookies

- 2/3 cup walnut halves and pieces (75 grams)
- 16 tablespoons unsalted butter (2 sticks/225 grams) at room temperature
- 1/3 of a cup (135 grams) sugar granules
- 1 large egg, plus 2 large egg yolks, beaten (for egg wash)
- 2/3 cup (290 grams) flour (all-purpose)
- kosher salt (1/2 teaspoon)

Method:

1. Follow these steps: Preheat the oven to 350 degrees and place a rack in the middle to make the cookies.
2. On a baking sheet, spread all of the walnuts (for the cookies and topping) and toast for 10 to 12 minutes, shaking the pan occasionally until fragrant and slightly darkened. To avoid overcooking the walnuts, place them on a plate. Finely chop once cool enough to handle.
3. 2 to 3 minutes on medium speed, scraping the bowl as needed, beat the butter and granulated sugar in the bowl of a stand mixer fitted with the paddle attachment or in a large mixing bowl with a hand mixer until light and fluffy. Add the egg yolks and beat on medium speed for 2 minutes, scraping the bowl a few times until the yolks are fully incorporated.
4. Mix in about two-thirds of the walnuts (75 grams), as well as the flour and salt, at low speed until the batter clumps together into a few large pieces. Remove the dough from the bowl and roll it out into a thick disk before wrapping it in plastic wrap. Refrigerate until firm, at least 1 hour or up to 3 days.
5. If you turn off the oven after toasting the nuts, preheat it to 350 degrees. Preheat oven to 350°F. Line two large, rimmed baking sheets with parchment paper.
6. Remove the dough from the refrigerator and cut it into small pieces, about the size of a golf ball. Each piece should be around 35 grams in weight, but you can make them smaller if you prefer. Refrigerate for 10 minutes after placing the balls on the lined baking sheets, spacing them a couple inches apart. (If you only have room in the refrigerator for one pan, chill the second batch while the first bakes.)
7. Combine the remaining walnuts, brown sugar, coconut, butter, and five-spice powder in a small bowl to make the topping.
8. Remove the shaped cookies from the refrigerator and brush them with beaten egg. Remove the cookies from the oven after 5 minutes and make a thumbprint in each one. Return to the oven for 15 to 18 minutes, rotating halfway through, until lightly golden, filling the thumbprint with about 1 teaspoon walnut streusel topping.
9. Allow the cookies to cool for a few minutes on the baking sheet before transferring to a wire rack to cool completely. Repeat the process with the second batch (you may have a little streusel left over depending on the yield and how big your thumbprints are).

GREEN TEA FORTUNE COOKIES

Prep Time: 10-20 minutes
Cooking Time: 60 minutes
Number of Servings: 18 Large Cookies

Ingredients:

- 3/4 cup of sugar
- 3 egg whites, large
- melted and cooled 4 ounces unsalted butter
- 1/2 cup flour (all-purpose)
- 1 tbsp green-tea powder (matcha)
- 18 small fortune cookies

Method:

1. Whisk the sugar, egg whites, butter, flour, and green-tea powder together in a medium mixing bowl until smooth. Refrigerate the batter for 1 hour, covered.
2. Preheat the oven to 325°F and place a silicone mat on a baking sheet. Make sure you have a coffee mug and a muffin tin on hand. Place two 2-tablespoon-sized mounds of batter 6 inches apart on the baking sheet. Spread the batter into two 6-inch rounds with an offset spatula.
3. Bake for 12 to 14 minutes in the center of the oven until the edges are browned, but the centers are still light. Allow cooling for 10 seconds before inverting one tuile and placing a paper fortune in the center with a spatula. Fold the tuile in half and then bring the ends together, forming a crease with the rim of the coffee mug.
4. To keep the fortune cookie's shape, place it in a muffin cup. Using the second tuile, repeat the process.
5. Return the tuile to the oven for a few seconds if it hardens. Using the remaining batter and fortunes, repeat the process. Before serving, allow the cookies to cool completely.

CHINESE MARBLE COOKIES

Prep Time: 10-20 minutes
Cooking Time: 11 minutes
Number of Servings: 24 Cookies

Ingredients:

- 2 room temperature butter sticks
- 3/4 cup of sugar
- 3/4 cup sugar (brown)
- 1 tsp vanilla extract
- 2 whole eggs
- 1 1/4 cup flour, plus 1/2 cup flour set aside
- 1/4 teaspoon of salt
- 1 tbsp baking soda
- 6 tablespoons cocoa powder

Method:

1. Preheat the oven to 375 degrees Fahrenheit.
2. Combine butter and sugars in a mixing bowl and beat until smooth.
3. Mix in the vanilla and eggs until well combined.
4. Mix in 1 1/4 cup flour, salt, and baking soda until everything is smooth.
5. The dough should be divided in half. To one-half, add the remaining 1/2 cup flour and mix until smooth.
6. To the remaining half, add the cocoa powder and stir until well combined.
7. Using a small cookie scoop, scoop the "vanilla" dough into balls (fill scoop a little less than halfway) and place it on parchment paper.
8. Proceed with the chocolate dough in the same manner.
9. Take one of each, press them together, flatten them into a fat disk, and liberally roll the edges in chocolate jimmies.
10. Place one inch apart on a baking sheet lined with parchment paper (I usually fit 7 per sheet).
11. Bake for approximately 11 minutes, or until done to your liking. You don't want the edges of the pizza to brown.
12. Allow cooling for a few minutes on the tray before transferring to a cooling rack to cool completely.
13. Enjoy in a cookie jar or an airtight container!

AWESOME PEANUT COOKIES

Prep Time: 10-20 minutes
Cooking Time: 20 minutes
Number of Servings: 4

Ingredients:

- 4 cups roasted peanuts, ground
- 1 cup sugar (powdered) (icing sugar)
- 1 quart of peanut oil
- 2 tbsp. vegetable shortening
- 2 cups flour (all-purpose)
- 1 egg yolk, lightly beaten for egg wash

Method:

1. Combine the ground peanuts, sugar, oil, shortening, and flour in a large mixing bowl. Form into small balls and place on a parchment paper-lined baking sheet.
2. Using the cap of your toothpaste, make a small circle pattern on the top of the peanut cookies. To make the circle, gently press the cap on top of each cookie.
3. Brush the tops of the peanut cookies with the egg wash and bake for 20 minutes at 350°F (180°C) or until golden brown.
4. Allow cooling after removing from the oven. The peanut cookies can be kept in an airtight container for up to two weeks.

WHIMSICAL CAKE AND FAMOUS CHINESE DESSERT RECIPES

THE GOOD OLD SACHIMA

Prep Time: 10-20 minutes
Cooking Time: 30 minutes
Number of Servings: 32 Medium Dumplings

Ingredients:

Noodle Dough
- 1/2 teaspoon salt
- /2 teaspoons, baking soda
- 2 large eggs
- 2 cups all-purpose flour
Syrup
- 6 maltose
- 1/2 cup water
- 1 cup white sugar
Others
- 1/4 cup cornstarch for dusting

Method:

1. Combine the all-purpose flour, brown sugar, and spice, and then stir in the egg fluid.
2. Combine all ingredients in a ball and whisk until smooth.
3. Allow the dough to rest for at least thirty minutes after covering it.
4. Heat the oil until it is extremely hot, then measure with one strip.
5. Tiny batches of strips should be fried until they are slightly orange. Shake off any excess oil before placing all of the strips in a big jar.
6. Add sugar, sucrose, salt, and water to a large saucepot.
7. Warm the fluid over a moderate flame until it reaches 115 degrees Celsius.
8. By streams, pour the fluid into the flour. Mix thoroughly, attempting to cover each strip in syrup.
9. Store toppings in airtight bags and store at room
10. temperature for up to 1 week.

ULTIMATE TASTY BANANA FRITTERS

Prep Time: 10-20 minutes
Cooking Time: 16 minutes
Number of Servings: 8

Ingredients:

- 1/2 cup hot water
- 3 teaspoons gelatin
- 1/3 cup white sugar
- 2 large ripe mangoes, peeled, pitted, and sliced
- 1 cup coconut milk

Method:

1. In a bowl, add the boiling water and gelatin and beat vigorously until dissolved.
2. Add the sugar and stir until dissolved.
3. In a food processor, add the mango and pulse until smooth.
4. Add the gelatin mixture and coconut milk and pulse until well combined.
5. Transfer the pudding into serving bowls and refrigerate for about 4-6 hours before serving.

AUTHENTIC MOONCAKE

Prep Time: 10-20 minutes
Cooking Time: 20 minutes
Number of Servings: 10

Ingredients:

Dough
- ½ cup golden syrup
- ¼ teaspoon kansui
- ¼ cup vegetable oil
- 1 cup cake flour

Filling
- 10 egg yolk, salted
- 2 cups lotus paste
- Egg wash to brush the cake

Method:

1. In a mixing bowl, carefully combine golden syrup, lye water, and vegetable oil.
2. Flour should be sieved. Toss everything into the mixture mentioned above at once.
3. Place the dough on a cling wrap sheet. Refrigerate the dough for thirty minutes to allow it to relax.
4. To remove the white that has stuck to the salted egg yolk, wash it with water. Allow airing to dry.
5. Wrap the lotus paste around the yolk.
6. After that, roll it up into a ball. Remove from the equation.
7. Between two plastic sheets or cling wraps, roll out the pastry.
8. Remove the cling film from the pastry and fold it toward the filling.
9. To ensure a consistent thickness, pinch away the excess pastry where the pastry is double folded.
10. To make a ball, roll the mooncake between your palms.
11. On a floured surface, roll out the mooncake.
12. Plunge the mold's piston into the flour, shaking off the excess.
13. Place the dough on the prepared baking sheet.
14. Place the mooncake mold on top of the dough and lower the piston. The dough will mold itself to the shape of the mold, leaving the pattern imprinted on the surface.
15. Bake for five minutes on the middle rack at 175°C/350°F top and bottom temperatures, or until the surface begins to firm up.
16. Remove the mooncake from the oven and brush the egg wash over the entire surface.
17. Cook for an additional ten minutes, or until golden brown.
18. Allow the cake to cool at room temperature after removing it from the oven.
19. Before serving, store the mooncake in an airtight container for three days.

SOY BEAN PUDDING

Prep Time: 10-20 minutes
Cooking Time: 15 minutes
Number of Servings: 6

Ingredients:

For Pudding
- 4 cups soy milk
- 1 tablespoon agar-agar powder
- 1/2 cup water
- 2 teaspoons vanilla extract

For Syrup
- 3/4 cup water
- 1/2 cup sugar
- 1 (1-inch) piece fresh ginger, smashed

Method:

1. For the pudding: In a medium pan, add soy milk over medium heat and cook for about 2-3 minutes or until warmed.
2. In another pan, add a Vz cup of water over medium heat and ring to a boil.
3. Add agar-agar powder and stir until dissolved.
4. Stir in the warm soy milk and vanilla extract and bring t a gentle boil, stirring continuously.
5. Remove from the heat and through a strainer, strain the mixture into a large pan.
6. With a clean kitchen towel, warp the lid tightly.
7. Then cover the pan with a lid and set it aside to cool slightly.
8. Refrigerate the pan for about 2 hours.
9. For the syrup: In a small pan, add all ingredients over medium heat and cook for about 3-5 minutes or until sugar is dissolved, stirring continuously.
10. Remove from the heat and discard the ginger.
11. Remove the pudding pan from the refrigerator and, with a flat spatula, cut it into thin slices.
12. Top with sugar syrup and serve.

TAPIOCA PUDDING

Prep Time: 10-20 minutes
Cooking Time: 35 minutes
Number of Servings: 6

Ingredients:

- 6 cups water, divided
- 1 and 1/2 pounds taro, peeled and cut into Vi inch pieces
- 1/2 cup tapioca pearls
- 1(13.7-ounce) can coconut milk
- 1 cup sugar

Method:

1. In a medium pan, add 4 cups of water and taro over high heat and bring to a boil.
2. Reduce the heat to medium and cook for about 20 minutes.
3. Remove from the heat and drain the water.
4. With a fork, mash the taro pieces slightly.
5. Meanwhile, in a small pan, add remaining water and bring to a boil.
6. Stir in the tapioca and cook for about 6 minutes.
7. Remove from the heat and set the pan aside, covered for about 10-15 minutes, or until the pearls are translucent.
8. Through a colander, strain the tapioca and rinse under cold running water.
9. Return the tapioca into the pan with coconut, taro, and sugar and mix well.
10. Place the pan over medium heat and cook for about 2-3 minutes or until sugar dissolves completely, stirring continuously.
11. Remove from the heat and set aside to cool slightly.
12. Serve either warm.

AMAZING SESAME BALL

Prep Time: 10-20 minutes
Cooking Time: 120 minutes
Number of Servings: 8 balls

Ingredients:

- 1/4 cup sesame seeds
- 4 cups peanut oil
- 1/4 cup room temperature water
- 7 ounces lotus paste
- 1 and 1/2 cups glutinous rice flour
- 1/2 cup boiling water
- 1/3 cup granulated sugar

Method:

1. To make the sesame ball flour, combine all of the ingredients in a mixing bowl.
2. In a mixing bowl, combine half a cup of glutinous rice sugar and flour.
3. Into the sugar and flour, pour VA cup boiling water. VA cup ambient temperature water and the remaining glutinous flour are added.
4. The mass of your coating should be half that of your dough ball.
5. Roll the ball in sesame oil that has been soaked until it is fully coated.
6. In a medium deep bowl, heat 4 cups almond or soybean oil to a comfortable 320°F.
7. In a small bowl, toss four sesame balls in the liquid.
8. Fry for the next five minutes, or till they turn a soft golden color, for a maximum of 17-18 minutes.
9. Place the completed sesame balls in a fine-mesh sieve, cooling rack, or sheet lined with towels to remove the oil.
10. Allow cooling for ten minutes before serving.

THE PERFECT MUNG BEAN CAKE

Prep Time: 10-20 minutes
Cooking Time: 60 minutes
Number of Servings: 32 Medium Dumplings

Ingredients:

- 1 cup sugar
- Pinch of salt
- ¼ cup butter
- ½ cup vegetable oil
- 2 cups yellow mung beans
- 1 teaspoon Matcha powder

Method:

1. The yellow mung beans should be pre-soaked overnight.
2. Add enough clean water to cover the mung beans in a medium-slow cooker partially.
3. Cook according to the bean method until the beans are light and easy to break.
4. Then, using a spoon, mash them together until you have a nice and fine blend. Place it in a nonstick skillet.
5. Toss the mung bean combination with a pinch of salt, oil, and cooking oil.
6. Heat over medium-low heat, stirring constantly.
7. When the oil has been fully absorbed, add the sugar.
8. Gradually stir till they can comfortably stick together. Switch the stove off.
9. Then, using a spatula, pass the solution to a filter.
10. If you want to have more, pour the dough into shorter doughs of 30g to 40g and cover ten fillings.
11. Use a mooncake mold or some other mold to shape the mooncakes.
12. This phase should be performed when the combination is warm and not hot.

THE ORIGINAL FA-GAO

Prep Time: 10-20 minutes
Cooking Time: 20 minutes
Number of Servings: 10 Cakes

Ingredients:

- 1/4 cup rice flour
- 1 tablespoon baking powder
- 1/4 cup neutral oil
- 1 and 1/4cups all-purpose flour
- 1/2 cup dark brown sugar

Method:

1. Position a 10-inch wooden or steel steamer bucket in a 12-inch pan or skillet filled with 2 inches of water.
2. In a food processor or blender, whisk together the brown sugar, oil, and 3A cup warm water until the sugar is dissolved, around 1 minute.
3. Scroll the all-purpose flour and com starch into the sugar syrup in three batches, stirring between each inclusion until no dry spots remain.
4. Fill the egg tart molds to the tip.
5. Under medium temperature, bring water in the pan to a gentle simmer.
6. Place the molds on a cooling rack to clear.
7. Repeat the bubbling process with the remaining five molds in the steamer basket.
8. Hot or at ambient temperature, prepare the cakes.

CLASSIC RED BEAN POPSICLES

Prep Time: 10-20 minutes
Cooking Time: 30 minutes
Number of Servings: 6

Ingredients:

- 25g caster sugar
- 100g sweet red bean paste
- 125ml cream
- 2 egg yolks
- 250ml milk

Method:

1. In a small saucepan, carry the milk and butter to a low boil.
2. Remove the pan from the heat and set it aside.
3. In a mixing bowl, whisk two egg yolks and sugars until the combination is light and moist.
4. Mix in the sweet red condensed milk with the glucose and yolk combination.
5. Load the warm wet ingredients into the beaten egg in a steady stream, constantly whisking until smooth.
6. Spoon the sauce into a large casserole dish and cook for five minutes on low heat, stirring constantly.
7. Freeze it in the refrigerator.
8. Fill an ice cream maker halfway with the chilled combination.
9. For about twenty minutes, run the ice cream machine.

JUICY DUMPLINGS

DUMPLING DOUGH RECIPE

Prep Time: 10-20 minutes
Cooking Time: 30 minutes
Number of Servings: 32 Medium Dumplings

Ingredients:

- 2 cups all-purpose flour Vz teaspoon salt (optional)
- 3/4 cup boiled water or cold water depending on the kind of dumpling you want to make. The fried dumpling is steamed then fried

Method:

1. Add flour and salt, if used, to a large mixing bowl.
2. Slowly add water to it.
3. After adding all of the water, start kneading the dough slowly.
4. If the dough isn't easy to knead, add some more water with a spoon.
5. Now transfer the dough onto a flat lightly-floured surface.
6. Knead it further to make a smooth and elastic dough.
7. Cover the dough in plastic wrap, and let it rest for 30 minutes before using.
8. You can refrigerate it and use it later for up to 3-4 days.

AUTHENTIC SHANGHAI DUMPLINGS

Prep Time: 40 minutes
Cooking Time: 20 minutes
Number of Servings: 32

Ingredients:

- 3 cups plus 2 tablespoons all-purpose flour
- 3/4 cup boiling water
- 1/4 cup cold water
- 1 tablespoon sunflower oil
  Filling ingredients
- 1 pound ground pork
- 1/2 pound shelled and deveined shrimp, finely chopped
- 3 green onions, finely chopped
- 2 teaspoons white sugar
- 2 tablespoons soy sauce
- 2 teaspoons fresh ginger, grated
- Salt and pepper

Method:

1. Add the flour to a food processor. Remove x/4 cup of it, and put it aside.
2. Add the boiling water slowly, and pulse until a stiff dough forms.
3. Add the cold water and the sunflower oil to it. Pulse until the dough becomes smooth and elastic. If it is too wet and sticky, add some of the reserved flour. Pulse the dough a few more times until the dough is smooth. You can also make the dough manually. Just make sure to knead enough until you have a smooth and elastic dough.
4. Wrap the dough in plastic wrap and let it rest for 30 minutes at room temperature.
5. In the meantime, make the filling. Add all the ingredients, one by one, to a large bowl. Season with salt and pepper. Mix thoroughly.
6. After half an hour has passed, divide the dough into 32 small, even pieces.
7. On a floured working surface, roll them using a rolling pin into very thin circular wrappers. Use a 4-inch round cookie cutter or a glass to make clean-cut wrappers.
8. Place the wrappers on a clean, lightly floured working surface.
9. Add 1 generous tablespoon of the filling to the center of the wrapper. Brush the edges of the wrapper lightly around the filling with some water. Bring all the edges over the filling and seal by pinching the dough together.
10. Prepare a bamboo steamer and steam the dumplings for 15 minutes.
11. Serve the dumplings hot with a dumpling dipping sauce.

CHICKEN AND LEEK DUMPLINGS

Prep Time: 15 minutes
Cooking Time: 10 minutes
Number of Servings: 16

Ingredients:

- 1 leek, chopped
- 2 cups roast chicken, chopped
- 1 cup shredded cabbage
- 1 tablespoon ginger root, grated
- 1/4 cup rice wine
- 1 teaspoon salt
- 2 tablespoons soy sauce
- 1 egg, beaten with 1 tablespoon of water Extra light olive oil
- 16 dumpling wrappers

Method:

1. Heat 3 tablespoons oil in a skillet, add leek, saute for a minute, and remove from heat.
2. Add roast chicken, cabbage, ginger root, rice wine, soy sauce, salt, and mix well.
3. Place a tablespoon of filling in the center of the dumpling wrapper, now brush the top half-circle edge with beaten egg.
4. Bring the bottom half up over the filling to meet the top half and pinch the two halves together all along the sides; give a second pinch over to ensure there are no air holes.
5. Place dumplings on a plate and cover them with a slightly damp cloth to ensure they do not dry out.
6. Fill a large pot of water up halfway over medium heat and bring to a boil.
7. Drop a batch of dumplings into the water and cook for 10 minutes. Leave raw dumplings under a damp cloth. You can also steam the dumplings for 12-15 minutes.
8. Warm 1-2 tablespoons of olive oil in a large skillet. Once the dumplings are cooked, fry them in small batches in the heated skillet until golden brown.
9. Serve warm with a dumpling dipping sauce.

CURRIED BEEF DUMPLING DELIGHTS

Prep Time: 15 minutes
Cooking Time: 20 minutes
Number of Servings: 18

Ingredients:

- 1 pound ground beef
- 1 red bell pepper, seeded, diced
- 1 green onion, minced
- 2 cloves garlic, minced
- 1 tablespoon ginger, grated
- 1 egg, beaten
- 1/4 cup low-sodium soy sauce 1 teaspoon black pepper
- 1 teaspoon curry powder Extra light olive oil
- 18 dumpling wrappers

Method:

1. Heat light olive oil in a skillet over medium heat.
2. Add beef, garlic, onion, and saute until beef is browned.
3. Add red bell pepper, ginger, soy sauce, black pepper, mix and remove from heat.
4. Place a tablespoon of filling in the center of the dumpling wrapper, now brush the top half-circle edge with beaten egg.
5. Bring the bottom half up over the filling to meet the top half and pinch the two halves together all along the sides; give a second pinch over to ensure there are no air holes.
6. Place dumplings on a plate and cover them with a slightly damp cloth to ensure they do not dry out.
7. Fill a large pot of water up halfway over medium heat and bring to a boil.
8. Drop a batch of dumplings into the water and cook for 10 minutes. Leave raw dumplings under a damp cloth. You can also steam the dumplings in a bamboo steamer for 12-15 minutes.

JUICY MUSHROOM DUMPLINGS

Prep Time: 10 minutes
Cooking Time: 15 minutes
Number of Servings: 14

Ingredients:

- 10 button mushrooms, chopped
- 1/2 cup bamboo shoots 1 cup green cabbage
- 1 green onion, minced
- 1 tablespoon ginger, grated
- 4 tablespoons low-sodium soy sauce
- 1 teaspoon black pepper Extra light olive oil
- 14 dumpling wrappers

Method:

1. Heat light olive oil in a skillet over medium heat.
2. Add mushroom, onion, garlic, and saute for a minute.
3. Add soy sauce, black pepper, bamboo shoots, and green cabbage, and remove from heat.
4. Place a tablespoon of filling in the center of the dumpling wrapper, then brush the top half-circle edge with your flour mixture.
5. Bring the bottom half up over the filling to meet the top half and pinch the two halves together all along the sides; give a second pinch over to ensure there are no air holes.
6. Place dumplings on a plate and cover them with a slightly damp cloth to ensure they do not dry out.
7. Fill a large pot of water up halfway over medium heat and bring to a boil.
8. Drop a batch of dumplings into the water and cook for 10 minutes. Leave raw dumplings under a damp cloth. You can also steam the dumplings in a bamboo steamer for 15 minutes.

PERFECT TRIFECTA DUMPLINGS

Prep Time: 15 minutes
Cooking Time: 20 minutes
Number of Servings: 14

Ingredients:

- 1/2 pound shrimp, peeled, deveined
- 1/2 pound pork
- 1/2 pound crab
- 3/4 cup green cabbage, shredded
- 1 green onion, minced
- 5 cloves garlic, grated
- 4 tablespoons low-sodium soy sauce
- 1 teaspoon black pepper Extra light olive oil
- 14 dumpling wrappers

Method:

1. Place shrimp and crab into a blender and mix into a paste.
2. Add pork into the shrimp mixture and mix.
3. Heat light olive oil in a skillet over medium heat.
4. Add garlic, onion, saute for 30 seconds. Add shrimp/crab/pork mixture and continue to saute until browned.
5. Add soy sauce, black pepper, and green cabbage. Mix and remove from heat.
6. Place a tablespoon of filling in the center of the dumpling wrapper, then brush the top half-circle edge with your flour mixture.
7. Bring the bottom half up over the filling to meet the top half and pinch the two halves together all along the sides; give a second pinch over to ensure there are no air holes.
8. Place dumplings on a plate and cover them with a slightly damp cloth to ensure they do not dry out.
9. Fill a large pot of water up halfway over medium heat and bring to a boil.
10. Drop a batch of dumplings into the water and cook for 8 minutes. Leave raw dumplings under a damp cloth. You can also steam the dumplings in a bamboo steamer for 10-15 minutes.

SPICED UP SHRIMP DUMPLINGS

Prep Time: 15 minutes
Cooking Time: 15 minutes
Number of Servings: 14

Ingredients:

- 3/4 pound shrimp, shelled, deveined
- 1 red chili pepper, seeded, chopped
- 1 red bell pepper, seeded, julienned
- 1 green onion, minced
- tablespoon ginger, grated
- 4 tablespoons low-sodium soy sauce
- tablespoons Sriracha
- 1 teaspoon black pepper
- 1 egg
- Extra light olive oil
- 14 dumpling wrappers

Method:

1. Heat light olive oil in a skillet over medium heat.
2. Add ginger, onion, saute for a minute.
3. Add shrimp and saute until pink.
4. Mix soy sauce, Sriracha, black pepper, and green cabbage with skillet mixture, remove from heat.
5. Place a tablespoon of filling in the center of the dumpling wrapper, then brush the edges with egg wash.
6. Bring the bottom half up over the filling to meet the top half, pinch the two halves together all along the sides, give a second pinch over to ensure there are no air holes.
7. Place dumplings on a plate and cover them with a slightly damp cloth to ensure they do not dry out.
8. Fill a large pot of water up halfway over medium heat, and bring to a boil.
9. Drop a batch of dumplings into the water and cook for 10 minutes. Leave raw dumplings under a damp cloth. You can also steam them for 15 minutes in a bamboo steamer.

CARAMELIZED SCALLION FRIED BEEF DUMPLING

Prep Time: 15 minutes
Cooking Time: 15 minutes
Number of Servings: 14

Ingredients:

- 1/4 pound ground beef
- 1 cup mung beans sprouts, roughly chopped
- scallions, finely chopped 1 tablespoon ginger, grated
- tablespoons low-sodium soy sauce 1 teaspoon black pepper
- 1 egg, beaten Extra light olive oil
- 14 dumpling wrappers

Method:

1. Heat light olive oil in a skillet over medium heat, add scallions, saute for 30 seconds.
2. Sprinkle scallions with brown sugar, give a quick saute.
3. Add ground beef and brown.
4. Add ginger, scallions, saute for a minute.
5. Add soy sauce, black pepper, mung bean sprouts, and green cabbage, mix and remove from heat.
6. Place a tablespoon of filling in the center of the dumpling wrapper. Brush the top half-circle edge with egg wash.
7. Bring the bottom half up over the filling to meet the top half, pinch the two halves together in the center, and then pinch the sides.
8. Place dumplings on a plate and cover them with a slightly damp cloth to ensure they do not dry out.
9. Fill a large pot of water up halfway over medium heat and bring to a boil.
10. Drop a batch of dumplings into the water and cook for 10 minutes. Leave raw dumplings under a damp cloth,
11. Warm 1-2 tablespoons of olive oil in a large skillet. Once the dumplings are cooked, fry them in small batches in the heated skillet until golden brown.
12. Serve warm with a dipping sauce like the spicy peanut sauce.

PEPPER PORK DUMPLINGS

Prep Time: 15 minutes
Cooking Time: 15 minutes
Number of Servings: 14

Ingredients:

- 3/4 pound ground pork
- 3/4 cup green cabbage 1 green onion, minced
- 1 tablespoon ginger, grated
- 4 tablespoons low-sodium soy sauce
- 1 teaspoon black pepper
- 1 egg, beaten Extra light olive oil 14 Dumpling wrappers

Method:

1. Heat light olive oil in a skillet over medium heat.
2. Add ground pork and brown.
3. Add ginger, onion, saute for a minute.
4. Add soy sauce, black pepper, and green cabbage, mix, and remove from heat.
5. Place a tablespoon of filling in the center of the dumpling wrapper, then brush the top half-circle edge with beaten egg.
6. Bring the bottom half up over the filling to meet the top half, pinch the two halves together all along the sides, and give a second pinch over to ensure there are no air holes.
7. Place dumplings on a plate and cover them with a slightly damp cloth to ensure they do not dry out.
8. Fill a large pot of water up halfway over medium heat and bring to a boil.
9. Leave raw dumplings under a damp cloth.
10. Place the dumpling in a prepared steamer and cook for 15 minutes.
11. Serve warm with your favorite dipping sauce.

JUICY PORK AND SHRIMP DUMPLINGS

Prep Time: 10-20 minutes
Cooking Time: 1 Hour
Number of Servings: 20 Pieces

Ingredients:

- 1/2 pound ground pork
- 8-10 medium shrimps, cooked and chopped finely
- 1 scallion stalk, finely chopped
- 1 teaspoon Shaoxing wine
- 1/2 teaspoon salt
- ½ teaspoon soya sauce
- 1/2 teaspoon sesame oil

Method:

1. Start with mixing all the dry ingredients and seasonings
2. With the mixture ready, you can now begin to fill in the dumplings.
3. Take a dumpling wrapper and place the mixture at the center.
4. Now wet the edges of the wrapper and fold the dumpling, making proper pleats.
5. Place them in a steamer and cook for 8-10 minutes.
6. Serve with a dipping sauce like the classic soy and vinegar dipping sauce.

CHINESE BREAKFAST DISHES AND DRINKS

STIR-FRIED EGG AND TOMATO

Prep Time: 10-20 minutes
Cooking Time: 7 minutes
Number of Servings: 4

Ingredients:

- 1 pound tomatoes, cut into small wedges
- 1 scallion, chopped finely
- 4 eggs
- 1 teaspoon Shaoxing wine
- 1./2 teaspoon sesame oil
- Salt, taste
- 1/4 ground white pepper
- 3 tablespoon vegetable oil, divided
- 2 teaspoons sugar
- 1/4- 1/2 cup water

Method:

1. In a bowl, add eggs, wine, sesame oil, salt, and white pepper and beat until well combined.
2. In a skillet, heat 2 tablespoons of oil over medium heat.
3. Add the egg mixture and cook for about 2 minutes, stirring continuously.
4. Transfer the scrambled eggs onto a plate and set them aside.
5. Heat the remaining oil over high heat in the same skillet and stir fry the tomatoes and scallions for about 1 minute.
6. Add sugar, salt, and water and stir to combine.
7. Stir in the cooked eggs and cook, covered for about 1-2 minutes or until the tomatoes are softened completely.
8. Uncover the skillet and stir fry for about 1-2 minutes or until the sauce thickens.
9. Serve hot.

CHINESE CHICKEN WINGS

Prep Time: 10-20 minutes
Cooking Time: 65 minutes
Number of Servings: 12

Ingredients:

- 2 tablespoons garlic powder
- 5 pounds of chicken wings
- 2 cups soy sauce
- 2 cups brown sugar

Method:

1. Mix all ingredients except chicken wings.
2. Heat ingredients until brown sugar melt completely.
3. Pour mixture over chicken wings and wrap the bowl with a plastic
4. cover.
5. Marinate chicken for 8 hours in the refrigerator.
6. Heat oven on 365°F.
7. Cover chicken with aluminum foil and bake for 45 minutes oven.
8. Remove foil and bake for 15 minutes more.
9. Serve hot with sauce

DELIGHTFUL CHICHEN CONGEE

Prep Time: 10-20 minutes
Cooking Time: 10 minutes
Number of Servings: 4

Ingredients:

- 8 cups water
- 1 cup long-grain white rice, rinsed and drained
- 6 bone-in chicken thighs
- 1(1 -inch) piece fresh ginger, sliced into large pieces
- Salt, to taste

Method:

1. In a large Dutch oven, add water, rice, chicken thighs, and ginger over high heat and bring to a boil.
2. Reduce the heat to medium-low and cook, covered for about 1 hour, stirring occasionally.
3. With a slotted spoon, transfer the chicken thighs into a bowl.
4. With 2 forks, shred the meat and discard the bones.
5. Add the shredded meat and salt into the rice mixture and stir to combine.
6. Serve hot.

CHINESE EGG ROLLS

Prep Time: 10-20 minutes
Cooking Time: 70 minutes
Number of Servings: 4

Ingredients:

- 8-ounce bamboo shoots
- 1 cup wood ear mushroom
- 4 teaspoons vegetable oil
- 3 large eggs
- 1 teaspoon sugar
- 14-ounce egg roll wrappers
- 1 egg white
- 1 pound roasted pork
- 2 green onions
- 2 1/2 teaspoons soy sauce
- 4 cups oil for frying
- 1 medium head cabbage
- 1/2 a carrot
- 1 teaspoon salt

Method:

1. 1 tbsp oil, heated in a skillet
2. Cook for 2 minutes on low heat after adding the beaten egg to the oil.
3. Cook for 1 minute on the other side.
4. Set aside to cool before slicing into thin strips.
5. In a skillet, heat the remaining ingredients with the vegetable oil until the vegetables are fully cooked.
6. Refrigerate for 1 hour after adding the sliced egg to the vegetables.
7. Place the vegetable mixture in a plastic wrapper.
8. Roll the plastic sheet until the top corners are sealed.
9. Cover with plastic wrap to prevent drying.

HAND-PULLED TASTY NOODLES

Prep Time: 10-20 minutes
Cooking Time: 90 minutes
Number of Servings: 4

Ingredients:

- 2 teaspoons chili oil
- 1/4 cup of soy sauce
- black sesame seeds.
- 1 Thai Chile
- 3 and 1/2 cups all-purpose flour
- 1/2 teaspoon kosher salt
- 1 green onion
- 4 teaspoons toasted

Method:

1. Mix flour and salt.
2. Add water and make the dough.
3. Rest the dough for 30 minutes and cut it into small pieces.
4. Pull these pieces into thin sticks.
5. Boil this for 10 minutes and rest aside.
6. Heat the skillet and add other ingredients to cook.
7. Add hand-pulled noodles and cook for more than 2 minutes.
8. Serve with sauces.

PERFECT SCALLION OMELET

Prep Time: 10-20 minutes
Cooking Time: 6 minutes
Number of Servings: 4

Ingredients:

- 6 large eggs, beaten
- 1/2 teaspoon Maggi seasoning
- Salt and ground white pepper, to taste
- 1/2 cup bean sprouts
- 1/4 cup carrot, peeled and grated
- 3 scallions, sliced
- 1 tablespoon vegetable oil

Method:

1. Add the eggs, Maggi seasoning, salt, and white pepper in a bowl and beat until well combined.
2. Add bean sprouts, carrots, and scallions and stir to combine.
3. In a large skillet, heat the oil over medium heat.
4. Add the egg mixture, and with the spatula, spread evenly.
5. Cook for about 3 minutes, tilting the pan occasionally to let the uncooked mixture flow underneath.
6. Carefully flip the omelet and cook for about 2-3 minutes or until the omelet is done completely.

CLASSIC SHRIMP FOO YOUNG

Prep Time: 10-20 minutes
Cooking Time: 7 minutes
Number of Servings: 4

Ingredients:

- 4 eggs
- 1 cup cooked small shrimp
- 8 ounces fresh bean sprouts
- 1/3 cup scallions, sliced thinly
- 1/4 teaspoon garlic powder
- 2 tablespoons vegetable oil
- 3 cups chicken broth
- 2 tablespoons soy sauce
- 2 tablespoons distilled white vinegar
- 2 tablespoons sugar
- 2 tablespoons

Method:

1. Add the eggs, shrimp, bean sprouts, scallions, and garlic powder in a bowl and mix until well combined.
2. In a skillet, heat the oil over medium heat.
3. Place about Vi cup of the egg mixture into the skillet and shape into a patty.
4. Cook for about 4 minutes per side or until golden brown.
5. Transfer the patty onto a plate.
6. Repeat with the remaining egg mixture.
7. In a saucepan, add the remaining ingredients and beat until well combined.
8. Place the pan over medium-low heat and cook for about 5 minutes or until the sauce thickens, stirring frequently.
9. Place the sauce over patties and serve.

FRESH MORNING PANCAKES

Prep Time: 10-20 minutes
Cooking Time: 10 minutes
Number of Servings: 12

Ingredients:

- 1/3 cups unbleached all-purpose flour, plus more for dusting
- 3/4 cup boiling water
- 1/2 cup cold water
- 1 tablespoon sesame oil, toasted

Method:

1. In a bowl, place the flour.
2. Slowly add the boiling water, stirring continuously until shaggy dough ball forms.
3. Place the dough ball onto a lightly floured surface and with your hands until smooth ball forms.
4. Cover the dough ball with a damp kitchen towel and set it aside at room temperature for at least 30 minutes.
5. Uncover the dough ball and again knead until smooth.
6. Place the dough ball onto a lightly floured surface and then roll into a 12-inch-long log.
7. With a sharp knife, cut the dough roll into 12 equal-sized pieces.
8. With lightly floured hands, flatten each dough piece into 2-inch rounds.
9. Spread oil on 1 side of each dough round.
10. Make a pair of dough rounds y pressing lightly oiled sides together.
11. Roll each dough pair into a 7-inch pancake with a floured rolling pin, flipping over now and again to roll evenly on both sides.
12. Heat an ungreased cast-iron skillet over medium-high heat and cook 1 pancake for about 1 minute or until lightly golden.
13. Carefully flip the pancake and cook for about 30 seconds or until lightly golden.
14. Transfer the pancakes onto a plate.
15. Carefully separate the pancake into 2 thin pancakes.
16. Repeat with remaining pancakes.
17. Serve warm.

AWESOME SCALION CREPE

Prep Time: 10-20 minutes
Cooking Time: 15 minutes
Number of Servings: 9

Ingredients:

- 3/4 cup all-purpose flour
- 1/2 teaspoon salt
- 1/8 teaspoon ground white pepper
- 1 cup water
- 3 medium eggs
- 2 scallions, chopped finely
- 2 tablespoon vegetable oil

Method:

1. In a mixing bowl, add flour, salt, and white and mix well
2. Add water and mix until well combined.
3. Add eggs and scallions and mix until smooth.
4. Heat a non-stick skillet over medium heat.
5. Add about 4 tablespoons of the mixture and with a spatula, spread in an even layer.
6. Cook for about 3 0-40 seconds or until golden brown.
7. Carefully flip the crepe and cook for about 3 0-40 seconds or until golden brown.
8. Repeat with the remaining mixture.
9. Serve warm.

MORNING MEATBALL CONGEE

Prep Time: 10-20 minutes
Cooking Time: 40 minutes
Number of Servings: 4

Ingredients:

- 1/2 pound ground pork
- 2 tablespoons fish sauce
- 1 tablespoon soy sauce
- Freshly ground white pepper, to taste
- 8 cups chicken broth
- 1 cup jasmine rice
- 1 lemongrass stalk, cut into 3-inch pieces, and crushed
- 5 dried red chiles, stemmed
- ½ cup vegetable oil
- 5 garlic cloves, sliced thinly
- 1/2 cup distilled white vinegar
- 1 Serrano chile, seeded and minced
- 1/2 teaspoon

Method:

1. In a bowl, add the pork, fish sauce, soy sauce, and a pinch of white pepper and mix until well combined.
2. Set aside for about 15-30 minutes.
3. In a cast-iron pan, add the broth, rice, and lemongrass pieces over medium-high heat and bring to a boil.
4. Reduce the heat to low and simmer partially, covered for about 25 minutes.
5. Meanwhile, heat a small skillet over medium heat and toast the dried chiles for about 3 minutes, stirring continuously.
6. Transfer the dried chiles to a spice grinder and grind until roughly powdered.
7. With paper towels, wipe out the skillet.
8. Heat the oil over low heat in the same skillet and cook the garlic for about 10 minutes or until caramelized, stirring frequently.
9. Transfer the garlic oil into a small bowl and set aside.
10. In another small bowl, add the vinegar, Serrano, and sugar and stir until the sugar is dissolved.
11. With a small ice cream scooper, make about 1-inch meatballs with the pork mixture.
12. Discard the lemongrass from the rice mixture and drop it in the meatballs.
13. Increase the heat to medium-high and simmer covered heat for about 10 minutes, stirring occasionally.
14. Serve hot.

AUTHENTIC CHINESE FIZZ

Prep Time: 5 minutes
Cook Time:10 minutes
Number of Servings: 4

Ingredients:

- Appleton Estate rum, 2 oz.
- 14 ounces Triple Sec 14 ounces Luxardo Maraschino liqueur 12 ounces lemon juice
- 12 ounces simple syrup
- 14 ounces grenadine
- 1 beaten egg white
- 1 teaspoon Angostura bitters
- 1 orange wedge (as a garnish)
- Syrup
- 1 cup water
- 1 cup sugar

Method:

1. Shake all of the ingredients dry, then shake again with ice. Double strain into an ice-filled fizz or highball glass. Serve with a straw and garnished with an orange wedge.
2. In a small saucepan, combine sugar and water. Warm up over medium-high heat. Stir occasionally until the sugar dissolves. Before using, allow to cool to room temperature and drizzle syrup on top.
3. Simple syrup can be stored in an airtight container in the refrigerator for up to two weeks.

CONCLUSION

Chinese cuisine is very rich and diverse, with eight different branches. Various cooking techniques make the food stand apart and have distinct tastes and aromas. Chinese cuisine focuses on making foods bright and rich in color, usually achieved by using different spices and herbs and diverse ingredients. Herbs and spices also give a variety of amazing aromas to Chinese foods, making them unique and soothing. Chinese cuisine focuses on providing nutritious and healthy foods by using natural ingredients.

Chinese baking can be quite different than Western baking. For one, it is typically done on the stovetop rather than the oven, and many different types of doughs can be used.

The most common type of dough is called "bao," a yeasted bread dough that requires rolling or using a mold to make small, round buns. There are also Chinese buns called "cha siu bao" steamed and filled with barbecue pork and hoisin sauce; these were introduced by early Chinese immigrants to America during the 19th century.

Different cultures have their own unique styles of cooking. The same is true with baking, as Chinese and Western baking often differ in a number of ways. In this article, we will look at some of those differences and see how they have developed over time.

In China, many different types of baked goods use rice flour as the main ingredient instead of wheat flour which is more common in the West. This makes Chinese baked goods gluten-free and healthier because rice is a whole grain and does not contain any gluten, which can cause digestive issues for those who have Celiac disease or other gluten-related conditions.

Pursuing Chinese Baking might seem a bit difficult at first, but believe me, when I say this, the effort will be worth it because each and every dish is a work of art!

Stay safe, and best wishes!

Printed in Great Britain
by Amazon